# WHO'S HORRIBLE IN HISTORY

TERRY DEARY

ILLUSTRATED BY MARTIN BROWN

SCHOLASTIC

To the horribly good designer, Richard Smith. MB

to El Cid

with love from the Moors

Scholastic Children's Books,
Euston House,
24 Eversholt Street,
London NW1 1DB, UK

A division of Scholastic Ltd
London ~ New York ~ Toronto ~ Sydney ~ Auckland
Mexico City ~ New Delhi ~ Hong Kong

Editorial Director: Lisa Edwards
Editors: Victoria Garrard, Stefanie Smith and Catriona Clarke

Published in the UK by Scholastic Ltd, 2009

Text copyright © Terry Deary, 2009
Illustrations copyright © Martin Brown, 2009
Colour by Rob Davis

ISBN 978 1407 10789 9

Printed and bound by Tien Wah Press Pte. Ltd, Singapore

2 4 6 8 10 9 7 5 3 1

# CONTENTS

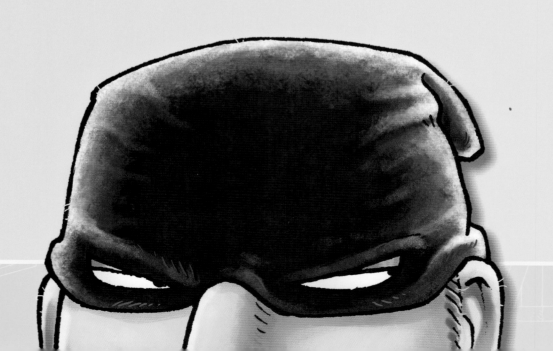

# INTRODUCTION

There are a few pleasant people in history. There is YOU for a start! You are probably one of the nicest people in the world!

You are probably the sort of person who gives your pet poodle the best dog food there is. You are such a saint you help old ladies to cross the road. You smile sweetly, even when you are suffering in history lessons ... and you shed salty tears when you run over a hedgehog on your bike.

There is a word for people like you...

No, the word is 'boring', I'm afraid. The only way kind, thoughtful and caring people end up in a history book is if something nasty happens to them. If an evil cook poisons your school dinner and kills you, then you'll become famous – dead famous.

We want to read about horrible people. People who help an old lady to cross the road ... but leave her in the path of a big, bruising bus. People who would aim for those hedgehogs as they ride their bike (with a spike). People who wouldn't feed their pet poodle the best dog food ... but they would sell the pooch to the dog-food factory to make mutt-flavour mincemeat.

Of course there have been millions of horrible people in history. There isn't a book big enough to fit them all in. THIS book will give you just 50 foul samples ... 50 ways of becoming horribly famous. Or 50 types of people to keep away from!

Who IS horrible in history? Read on...

# AWFUL ASSASSINS

If you're a leader then your enemies are dangerous, but your friends are far more deadly. People who kill leaders are called assassins.

## MARCUS JUNIUS BRUTUS (85–42 BC)
## VICTIM: ROMAN LEADER, JULIUS CAESAR

One of the most famous assassins in history was Brutus – Julius Caesar's so-called 'friend'. Brutus had fought against Caesar but was captured. Brutus said, 'Sorry', and Caesar not only forgave him, he made Brutus governor of Gaul. He trusted Brutus. Oh dear…

CAESAR? GREAT BLOKE. ROMAN LEADER … AND MY MUM'S BOYFRIEND. SHAME HE HAD TO DIE

HE GOT TOO BIG FOR HIS BOOTS – RED BOOTS! AS YOU KNOW, RED BOOTS ARE WORN BY KINGS – AND ROMANS DON'T LIKE KINGS

BOO

MY WIFE'S DAD, CATO, CAME UP WITH A PLOT TO KILL CAESAR WHEN WE ALL MET ON 15 MARCH. IT'S WHAT THE WIFE WANTED…

LOVELY!

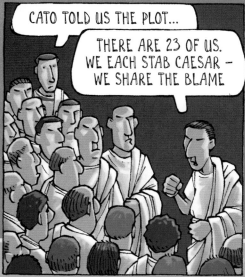

CATO TOLD US THE PLOT…

THERE ARE 23 OF US. WE EACH STAB CAESAR – WE SHARE THE BLAME

I WAS THE LAST TO GO. MY FRIEND CAESAR LOOKED AT ME AND SAID…

YOU TOO BRUTUS?

HE COVERED HIS FACE, I STABBED HIM IN THE GROIN, AND HE DIED IN A PUDDLE OF BLOOD … A SORT OF BLUDDLE! AND I CUT MY POOR LITTLE HAND

# FOUR FUNNY FACTS

**1** Caesar's assassins got in one another's way and stabbed each other. Poor Brutus cut his hand.

**2** We're not sure if Caesar really did say 'You too Brutus?' But Brutus may have cried 'Sic semper tyrannis!' as he struck. Or, 'That's what happens to tyrants!'

**3** Brutus has always been a hero to some people. In 1790s America the Booth family named their son Brutus Booth. Brutus Booth's son, John Wilkes Booth, went on to assassinate President Abraham Lincoln. As he shot him he cried, 'Sic semper tyrannis!'

**4** One of the assassins, Cassius, really hated Caesar. Caesar had pinched the lions Cassius kept for gladiator fights. The lions were set free to attack Cassius ... but instead they munched and crunched the peasants in the city.

> OI! CAREFUL! YOU COULD HURT SOMEONE WITH THAT

> I'VE GOT A SICK TEMPER

## STICKY END

The assassins let Caesar's very best friend live. He was called Mark Antony, and he raised an army to plot Caesar's revenge. A story says Brutus was visited by a devil who said, 'We'll meet again at Philippi'. Mark Antony and Brutus met in battle ... at Philippi. Brutus's army was beaten in battle and he killed himself. There is a story that Brutus's head was taken to Rome and thrown on the floor beside Caesar's statue.

ha ha

boo hoo

## FOUL FACT

BRUTUS'S BODY WAS BURNED (BUT NOT THE HEAD). THE ASHES WERE SENT TO HIS MUM ... HOW SWEET. BRUTUS'S WIFE PORTIA HEARD HE'D DIED SO SHE KILLED HERSELF! NEVER MIND, THE GRAVE-DIGGERS OF ROME WERE KEPT BUSY.

> MURDERS, REBELLIONS, EXECUTIONS, GLADIATORS, SUICIDES, ASSASSINATIONS... I LOVE THIS TOWN!

# Eadric Streona (died 1017)
## Victim: King Edmund II of England

Assassins have a dirty, low-down job to do, so THEY need to get dirty and low down to do it.

I'M ENGLISH ... BUT I QUITE LIKE THE INVADERS FROM DENMARK. I SWITCH SIDES TO MAKE SURE I AM ON THE WINNING TEAM. THE SAXONS PAY THE VIKINGS GOLD TO STAY AWAY ... AND SOME OF THAT GOLD ENDS UP IN MY PURSE

NOW KING EDMUND II WANTS ME TO FIGHT THE DANES. THAT DOES NOT SUIT ME ... OR MY PURSE. HE HAS TO GO

LET'S DECK THE DANES

YAY!

HE HAS LOTS OF BODYGUARDS, OF COURSE. SO WHERE DO I GET HIM ALONE? IN THE TOILET, OF COURSE...

THE TOILET IS A PIT IN THE GROUND. WHEN EVERYONE IS DRUNK AT THE FEAST, I SNEAK OUT AND HIDE IN THE TOILET PIT

POO

WHEN EDMUND SITS OVER THE PIT, I TAKE MY SWORD AND JAB HIM IN THE BUM. OOOOH I BET THAT HURTS!

CKKK

RESULT? ONE DEAD KING ... AND ME COVERED IN PIT. I'M OFF TO GET MY REWARD FROM THE DANES

# FOUR FUNNY FACTS

**1** Some stories say Eadric used a crossbow to shoot an arrow up the king's bum. The arrow went in so far they couldn't get it out. He was buried with the arrow. But there were no crossbows in England at that time. It was a lie.

**2** Eadric was a real rat. He changed sides from English to Danish when it suited him. At the Battle of Ashingdon he was fighting for King Edmund II ... yet he chopped off an English soldier's head and held it in front of the English army! He cried out, 'Run for your lives! Edmund is dead!' The real King Edmund ripped off his own helmet and called out, 'No I'm not! Fight on'.

**3** Eadric was called 'Streona', which meant 'grasping' or 'greedy' at the time.

**4** In the year 1002 Eadric took part in the St Brice's Day Massacre. Every Dane in England was to be murdered ... even the women and babies.

## STICKY END

Eadric played chess against his friend, King Canute of the Danes. He beat the king. Big mistake! They argued. Eadric cried, 'I killed Edmund II for you. You should pay me!'

Angry Canute said, 'I will raise you higher than any man in the land'. He turned to his bodyguard and said, 'Pay the man what we owe.'

The bodyguard paid Eadric with a killer blow from his war axe. His head was sliced off in one go.

## FOUL FACT

EADRIC'S HEAD WAS STUCK ON A POLE AND PLACED ON LONDON BRIDGE. AS CANUTE PROMISED, EADRIC WAS 'HIGHER THAN ANY MAN IN THE LAND'. HIS BODY WAS THROWN INTO THE RIVER THAMES AND LEFT TO ROT.

# WILLIAM DE TRACY (DIED ABOUT 1174)
## VICTIM: THOMAS BECKET, ARCHBISHOP OF CANTERBURY

Don't make a habit of arguing with your boss … and never argue with four men carrying huge swords.

I'M A NORMAN KNIGHT AND TRUE TO MY KING — THAT'S HENRY II, OF COURSE

THE KING WAS REALLY UPSET BY THE ARCHBISHOP OF CANTERBURY, THOMAS BECKET. BECKET SAID HIS CHURCH HAD POWER OVER THE KING OF ENGLAND

SO THERE!

HENRY WAS SPITTING FEATHERS. ONE NIGHT THE KING SHOUTED AT US...

WHO WILL GET RID OF THIS PROBLEM PRIEST FOR ME?

THUMP!

THUMP!

ME AND THREE OTHER LADS THOUGHT, 'HELLO! HE MEANS KILL TROUBLE-MAKER TOM!' SO WE SHARPENED OUR SWORDS AND SET OFF FOR CANTERBURY

HUGH DE MORVILLE CHOPPED OFF THE TOP OF HIS SHAVED NODDLE AND RICHARD LE BRETON SLICED INTO THE HOLY BRAINS

REGINALD FITZURSE GOT THE FIRST CHOP IN AND THE REST OF US PILED ON IN. TOM FELL AND WE KEPT CHOPPING

CHOPPY CHOP

THEN WE RAN...

# FOUR FUNNY FACTS

**1** In the struggle, one of Becket's clerks, Edward Grim, had his arm almost cut off. Bet he felt really grim after that.

**2** After Becket's murder, it was said:

A terrible storm cloud appeared, rain fell and the thunder rolled round the heavens, then the sky turned a deep red … a sign of the blood which had been shed.

**3** It was said that miracles started to happen. A blind man came to the cathedral, had his eyes touched with Thomas Becket's blood and he could see again. There would be bits of brain mixed with the blood, of course. Tasty.

**4** Thomas Becket was made a saint and people went to visit the place he had been hacked. Tom's bones were destroyed by another King Henry – Henry VIII – who didn't like bits of saints and all that sort of stuff. There are still a few Becket bones around the world, and some of Tom's clothes are still making miracles.

## FOUL FACT

BECKET'S ASSASSINS KILLED HIM. BUT A LOCAL MAN TURNED TOM INTO A REAL MESS. A REPORT SAID:

Then Hugh of Horsea planted his foot on Becket's neck and with the point of his sword drew out the blood and brains from the gash of the skull, scattering them on the pavement.

## STICKY END

The knights were told to say sorry. William de Tracy was sent to the Holy Land to fight in the Crusades and say sorry in Jerusalem. But the winds were so strong he was blown back. He failed.

That meant, when he died, he would probably go to Hell (and without his sword he'd have a devil of a time getting out).

BAD KNIGHTS SLEEP HERE

MY SWORD IS BRAINY!

# GUY FAWKES (1570–1606)
## VICTIM: KING JAMES I OF ENGLAND

Guy Fawkes wasn't happy with killing a king – he wanted to get rid of his lousy lords at the same time!

YES, I SET OUT TO BLOW UP KING JAMES AND HIS LORDS ON 5 NOVEMBER 1605. HE ASKED FOR IT

I'M A ROMAN CATHOLIC, AREN'T I? WHAT DOES JAMES DO TO CATHOLICS? TORTURES THEM AND EXECUTES THEM

SO WE LOADED THE CELLARS OF THE HOUSES OF PARLIAMENT WITH GUNPOWDER AND WAITED FOR JAMES TO ARRIVE

BUT JUST BEFORE MIDNIGHT A GUARD FOUND ME AND I WAS ARRESTED. THEY TOOK ME TO JAMES

OI!

I REFUSED TO TELL HIM WHO WAS IN ON THE PLOT WITH ME. SO JAMES SAID...

TORTURE HIM TILL HE TALKS

THEY STRETCHED ME ON THE RACK. AFTER DAYS OF TORTURE I SCREAMED THE NAMES THEY WANTED. THEN THEY EXECUTED ME ... HORRIBLY

EEK!

IT HURT

# FOUR FUNNY FACTS

**1** Guy was caught at least 12 hours before parliament was due to meet the king. And it wasn't 'luck'. The soldiers who caught Guy had been tipped off and were searching for explosives when they found him there. King James had also been tipped off. He was never in any real danger from the Gunpowder Plot.

**2** James still wanted to get rid of the Catholic priests. One plotter said that Father Henry Garnet was part of the plan to murder James. So this Catholic priest was also tortured and brought to trial. He was found guilty, of course, and sentenced to be hanged, drawn and quartered.

**3** It was sometimes hard to find anyone to execute victims like Guy. A report from Lancaster a few years later said...

No man could be persuaded to carry out the execution except a butcher. But he was so ashamed to do the job himself that he paid a servant five pounds to do it for him. The servant, however, took the money then ran away. He was replaced as executioner by a deserter from the army, who came to be detested by the good people of Lancaster.

**4** Funniest fact of all? People have bonfire parties with fireworks on 5 November every year. It's a flaming party for James being saved. But of course Guy Fawkes was caught BEFORE midnight on 5 November. So really we should be singing, 'Remember, remember the FOURTH of November'.

## STICKY END

As an example to others, an execution for treason was super-horrible. After hanging the victim for a few moments he was cut down, still alive, his naughty bits were chopped off and thrown on to a fire. Then he was slit open and his guts were thrown on to the fire. Finally he was beheaded and cut into quarters.

Guy cheated the executioner. When the rope was placed round his neck he jumped off the ladder and broke his neck. He was dead when they cut him open.

## FOUL FACT

WHEN GUY FAWKES WAS CAUGHT, HE WAS TAKEN TO A ROOM IN 'THE KING'S HOUSE' OF THE TOWER OF LONDON. THIS 'HOUSE' WAS BUILT IN HENRY VIII'S REIGN FOR THE TOWER'S GOVERNOR TO LIVE IN. KING HENRY'S SECOND WIFE, ANNE BOLEYN, SPENT HER LAST NIGHT IN THAT ROOM BEFORE SHE HAD HER HEAD CUT OFF THE NEXT MORNING. FOR MANY YEARS AFTER THE GUNPOWDER PLOT, SOLDIERS SWORE THAT GUY FAWKES HAUNTED THAT ROOM.

DID YOU HEAR SOMETHING?

IT'S JUST THAT GHOST GUY

# GAVRILO PRINCIP (1894–1918)
## VICTIM: ARCHDUKE FRANZ FERDINAND OF AUSTRIA-HUNGARY

The world's deadliest assassin killed 20 million people … with just one bullet.

I AM A PROUD MEMBER OF THE BLACK HAND GANG. WHAT DO WE WANT?

FREEDOM FOR SERBIA!

HOW WILL WE GET IT?

KILL OUR AUSTRIAN INVADERS … STARTING WITH ARCHDUKE FRANZ FERDINAND

THERE WERE SEVEN OF US IN ON THE PLOT. FERDI WAS DUE TO DRIVE THROUGH SARAJEVO. WE WERE ARMED WITH GUNS AND BOMBS AT DIFFERENT PARTS OF THE ROUTE

YOUNG ABRINOVI THREW HIS BOMB AT FERDI'S CAR…

FERDI PICKED IT UP AND THREW IT OUT OF HIS CAR. THE BOMB BLEW UP A FOLLOWING CAR AND INJURED EIGHT INNOCENT PEOPLE

BOOM

FERDI HEADED FOR THE HOSPITAL TO VISIT THE BOMB VICTIMS. BUT BY AN AMAZING CHANCE HIS DRIVER TOOK A WRONG TURNING. THIS ROAD TOOK HIM STRAIGHT TO ME

I SHOT FERDI AND HIS WIFE. FERDI'S UNCLE, THE EMPEROR OF AUSTRIA WAS FURIOUS. HE WANTED REVENGE AGAINST ALL OF SERBIA'S ALLIES

BANG

HE WANTED WAR

Austria blamed Serbia for the killing. The Austrians declared war on Serbia. Austria's friend, Germany, helped Austria. Russia helped Serbia … so France helped Russia. Germany marched through Belgium to get to France, so Britain joined in to help Belgium.

The frightful First World War had started. It was expected to last about four months but lasted four years. Twenty million people died … all from one shot by Gavrilo Princip.

# FOUR FUNNY FACTS

**1** Six Black Hand assassins were caught by Austria-Hungary. The leader, Danilo Ilic, was hanged. The other five were under 20 years old and so were just sent to prison.

**2** The young man who failed with the bomb, Abrinovi, swallowed poison and jumped in the river Miljacka to drown rather than be captured. But the crowd dragged him out of the river and saved him … then they nearly beat him to death!

**3** Back in 1853, someone had tried to kill the emperor of Austria, Franz Ferdi's Uncle Joe (it seems that family just weren't very popular). A man ran up to Joe and struck him in the neck with a knife. But Emperor Joe had a high army collar made of thick material. It saved his life.

**4** Franz Ferdi was also struck in the throat, just like Uncle Joe. But when doctors tried to unfasten his coat to stop the bleeding they couldn't. Fat Franz Ferdi had been stitched into the coat to make him look thin. By the time they cut the coat open he was dead. See? Obesity can be deadly.

*IT'S NOT MY FAULT – I WAS STITCHED UP!*

## STICKY END

*Gavrilo Princip was taken alive. He was allowed to live, but locked away. Just as the Great War reached an end, gunman Gavrilo died in prison of a lung disease.*

## FOUL FACT

THE DUCHESS HEARD TWO SHOTS, THEN SAW BLOOD SPURT FROM HER HUSBAND'S MOUTH. SHE CRIED, 'FOR HEAVEN'S SAKE! WHAT HAPPENED TO YOU?' SHE DIDN'T KNOW THAT THE FIRST SHOT HAD HIT HER IN THE STOMACH. A MOMENT LATER SHE FELL WITH HER FACE ON FRANZ FERDI'S KNEES AND DIED BEFORE HE DID.

# MANIC MONARCHS

Kings and queens are usually born to rule. But not many of them are fit to rule.

## EMPEROR COMMODUS (AD 161–192)

Some manic monarchs are a danger to everyone – and even to ostriches and crocodiles…

# ROMAN·EXPRESS

## WIN
### TICKETS TO SATURDAY'S BIG GAME

| The VENICE CHRISTIANS | v | The ROMAN LIONS |

## CAN I KILL MY SLAVE?
**ONE READER'S DILEMMA**

OUR EXPERT SAYS 'YES'

## FREE PEE
WASH YOUR CLOTHES THE ROMAN WAY WITH OUR UNBEATABLE URINE OFFER!

# COMMODUS COPS IT

Emperor Commodus died yesterday and Rome is a happy place today. He will be remembered for his love of the Roman 'Games'. In one day, it is said, Commodus killed five hippopotamuses with his bare hands. That's five unhappy hippos.

When it came to running the empire, Commodus had the help of a brilliant slave called Cleander. But even Cleander couldn't prevent the shortage of wheat that left the people hungry in the year AD 189.

A mob marched on Commodus's palace. He was doomed! He could fight five hippopotamuses but hippopotamuses don't carry swords and spears to fight back (at least not when they're in the circus).

Commodus hippo hunter

What could Commodus do? He met the mob and stood alongside the faithful Cleander.

'I know you're angry. But, let me tell you … it is all the fault of Cleander here!'

## SLAUGHTER

The mob believed the evil Emperor. They grabbed Cleander and hacked off his head. It didn't get the mob any more wheat, but they went home happy and Commodus was saved.

But not for long … by AD 192 Commodus, who was a few brain cells short of being a halfwit, started to think that he was the ancient god Hercules, returned to Earth. He ran the country in his spare time. But most of his hours were spent watching animals and chained

men slaughter one another in the arena. Gladiators with bows and arrows, spears and daggers would be set against wild animals – fresh crocodiles from Africa and elephants from India. Commodus himself beheaded ostriches with arrows.

Other victims would be tied to the bellies of wild boar to be kicked and gored to death by the beasts. Special victims had their clothes set alight.

Commodus saved the worst for Christians – women were gored by wild cows with sharpened horns, while Christian men were placed on hot iron seats till the crowd could smell their flesh roasting.

## COWARD

His Highness was a coward, of course. At one show he had 100 bears put in the arena. He then climbed on to a platform where the bears couldn't reach him. He threw spears or fired arrows till all the bears were dead.

While Commodus played, the work of ruling Rome was left to the consuls. Useful men to have around. Yet Commodus decided they should all be killed as a sacrifice to the gods.

The consuls decided to get him first. They hired an athlete to go into Commodus's bathroom and strangle him. Luckily the athlete succeeded, otherwise he'd have been for the high jump.

Emperor teddy tamer

In days of danger you need a tough monarch. You do not need someone who trusts their enemies and falls for a simple trick.

**1/64p**

## BRITISH SUN
AD 460 (ish)

### BATTLE OF THE BARDS
OUR BARDS-IN-THEIR-EYES FINALISTS

### FIGHTING FASHION WEEK
WHAT'S HOT IN THE COMBAT ZONE AND WHAT'S NOT
pages 3, 4, 5, 9, 11, 13, 19, 23 & 31

MORE INSIDE

# VORTIGERN TURNS UP HIS TOES

**WE SAY GOODBYE TO OUR HAS-BEEN HERO**

**K**ing Vortigern of the Britons died yesterday … a few years too late to save Britain.

When the Romans left Britain 20 years ago the great Vortigern took charge. This cunning king faced invasions from all sides. He simply used one invader to fight another. He arranged for Cunedda of the Gododdin tribe to settle in North Wales to resist the invasions of the Irish.

So where did it all go wrong?

A while later, the Monk Gildas said, 'To hold back the Pict enemies from Scotland he brought in those vile, unspeakable Saxons, led by brothers Hengest and Horsa. These Saxons are hated by God and humans alike. Nothing more frightful has happened to this island, nothing more bitter.'

### DEMANDING SAXONS

The Saxons did a good job but our visitors turned nasty and demanded a lump of Brit land for themselves. As Gildas explained: 'The Saxon barbarians grew in number. They demanded the food and clothing that Vortigern promised but the British people said, "We cannot feed and clothe you, for your numbers are grown. Go away, for we do not need your help."'

Hengest didn't just bring more warriors. He brought a secret weapon: his daughter! Vortigern fell for her and gave her father half of our kingdom.

Gildas wrote: 'All the great towns fell to the Saxon battering rams. Bishops, priests and people were all chopped down together while swords flashed and flames crackled. It was horrible to see the stones of towers thrown down to mix with pieces of human bodies. Broken altars were covered with a purple crust of clotted blood. There was no burial except under ruins and bodies were eaten by the birds and beasts.'

**BODY BITS**

**BIRDS**

**BEASTS**

### PARTY TIME

Then, on 24 August AD 456, St Bartholomew's Day, Hengest invited Vortigern to a feast. 'Bring along your top generals, no weapons though,' he said. 'We'll have a bit of a party – some ale, a few nibbles and a bit of a jolly singsong!'

The clue was there, wasn't it? St Bartholomew was that missionary chap who went to Africa to convert the pagans. They skinned him alive and chopped off his head. So one ought to have guessed that it wasn't a good evening to meet the jolly old pagan enemy.

Sure enough, Vortigern arrived with all the top lords in Britain – his best warriors, best ministers and best bishops. What did the savage Saxons do? Why they sat them down at the tables, waited till they were munching on the nibbles and then Hengest cried out, 'Saxons! Draw your knives!' They drew their great knives that they'd hidden in their boots!

### BLOOD BATH

It was all over in seconds. They killed the British lords. Blood all over the tables. Blood all over the rushes on the floor. The only one they left alive was Vortigern. He was made a prisoner and he had to give horrible Hengest quite a lot of land just to spare his life.

He survived but was hated by everyone. In the end Vortigern wandered from place to place till his heart broke and he died without honour.

Not many Brits will be sorry to see him go.

Some monarchs fall ill while they are on the throne. Good kings become sick kings and the people have to suffer them.

# FRENCH  TIMES

OCTOBER 1422

*1 GROAT*

# Charles hops the twig

**C**harles VI is dead and the people of France are not too sad.

The young king started off his rule so well. His coronation in 1380 turned out to be quite a party. Three great lords rode on horses to serve the 12-year-old King Charles VI. In the streets fountains ran with water, milk and wine.

There were reports of a bit of bother at the party. The Duke of Anjou and the Duke of Burgundy BOTH thought they should sit next to the new king. They scrambled and scrapped for the seat like two kids. The king's council said 'Burgundy should have it.' Anjou said 'I'm having it anyway' and sat down. He had to be dragged off.

But in April 1392 Charles suffered from a strange illness that caused his hair and nails to fall out. When Pierre de Cranon tried to murder Charles's friend Olivier de Clisson, Charles set off on a revenge attack. Big mistake. Charles was still ill. On a hot day in August Charles was riding at the front of his troop of knights, when a wild-looking man ran up to his horse and spoke some words of doom and terror. Soon after, a page dropped a lance.

The clatter scared Charles, who rushed forward with his sword drawn, and killed four of his own men before his knights could stop him. Charles lay on the ground, his eyes rolling from side to side. His servants found an ox-cart to carry him home.

After two days he felt a little better. When the king heard that he had killed four of his own knights, he wept. From then on his mind grew more and more sick.

## FLAMIN' FANCY DRESS

On 28 January 1393 Queen Isabeau gave a fancy-dress ball and Charles VI and a group of his friends dressed up like 'wild men' in linen costumes. They were accidentally set alight by a torch and four of them burned alive. Charles was saved by the Duchess of Berry, who threw her heavy skirts over him. The Queen fainted in terror.

The accident made Charles's illness worse and by June he was insane. A surgeon

**Quick-thinking Duchess of Berry**

drilled some holes in Charles's skull, hoping to cure him. Although Charles felt a little better after that he grew worse again in 1395. Some churchmen thought that Charles was the victim of witchcraft. Charles cried out: 'If there is any one of you who is a witch I beg him to torture me no longer but let me die!'

## FROM MAD TO WORSE

When he was ill Charles thought that his name was Georges. He said he was NOT the king and had no wife or any children. He ran from room to room until he dropped, worn out. He smashed the furniture and peed in his clothes. He attacked doctors and servants who tried to help him.

Charles started to believe that he was made of glass and that if people came too near him he would break. He said that iron rods should be slipped into his clothes to save him from breaking.

By 1405 Charles refused to change his clothes, to have a bath or a shave. He began to stink, had skin trouble and lice. He wandered through the palace, howling like a wolf. His doctors hoped to cure Charles with shock treatment. They arranged for some men to blacken their faces and hide in his room. When the King entered they all jumped out, shouting, 'Boo!' It worked! Charles agreed to be washed, shaved and dressed and for a few weeks he was better.

Charles VI died in Paris and everyone is happier ... even Charles.

Some monarchs are born too weak to rule. But because their dad was king they become king. Not all weak kings bring misery, though.

## AUSTRIAN MIRROR

1 pfennig • June 1875

**WIN A FREE NEWSPAPER WORTH 1 PFENNIG**

### ZODIAC SUDOKU

with Maria Von Toft

**WHAT DO THE NUMBERS SAY ABOUT YOU?**

# FERDINAND PUSHING UP DAISIES

**FROM OUR ROYAL COURT CORRESPONDENT**
Illma Keitup

Emperor Ferdinand is dead and Austria is a little sad.

As Ferdy once said: 'It is easy to rule, but what is difficult is to sign your name.' He wasn't the brightest kid on the block.

His idea of fun was to squash himself into a wastepaper basket and roll over and over like a ball. Ferdinand was an ugly child, with a large head, a flat skull and water on the brain. His face was

**INSIDE TODAY • NEWS • ENTERTAINMENT • GOSSIP • MORE GOSSIP • SPORT • AND GOSSIP**

not too pretty, with fat lips and a huge nose. His legs and arms were short and he couldn't keep hold of heavy objects, like a full cup or a bottle. One of Ferdinand's sisters, Marianna (1804–1858), was so ugly she was usually kept locked in a room.

Little Ferdinand was called 'Nandle' by his loving parents. His dad, Emperor Franz, played with his ugly son and gave little Nandle rides in a wheelbarrow through Laxenburg Park.

In 1831 Ferdy married Maria Anna of Sardinia, who was a nurse more than a wife. Ferdinand would stand for hours at his window, staring down at passers-by. Either that or he would play with his musical boxes. He was mainly interested in coats of arms and collected 5,000 shields. Once, an eagle was shot during a hunt. Ferdinand said that it could not be an eagle, because it had only one head — the eagle on his family shield had two.

In 1835 Ferdy's dad died and he became emperor. The prime minister ruled while Ferdinand rambled round the palace in a general's uniform with an umbrella tucked under his arm. The queen of Russia called him an 'oaf' but he was happy enough. As he always said, it was a good life.

NANDLE'S NEST

MINGIN' MARIANNA

MISERABLE MARIA ANNA

DEAD DAD FRANZ

NEPHEW FRANCIS

## 'I am Emperor, I want dumplings, so I get them.'

In 1848 the people of Austria started a revolution. Ferdinand was surprised. 'Are they allowed to do that?' he asked.

In the end he was driven out and he handed the throne to young Francis Joseph. He did it with no hard feelings and went off to live in Castle Hradschin in Prague. He grew very rich and lived happily ever after ... till he died.

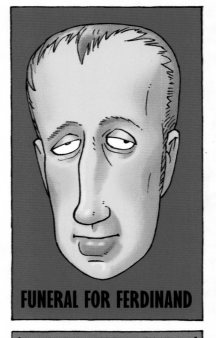

FUNERAL FOR FERDINAND

HAVE THE MIRROR DELIVERED EVERY DAY — STRAIGHT TO YOUR HOVEL

# Queen Victoria (1819–1901)

Some monarchs start out well but just go on too long. They go on till they are bored – and the whole country is bored with them.

## VICTORIAN  MAIL

WE ARE NEVER AMUSED · CHEAP

JANUARY 1901

### HOW TO RID YOUR ESTATE OF PESKY WILDLIFE
In our weekly hunting & countryside pull-out 'Horse, Hound & Wife' Part 16 tomorrow

# VICTORIA FINALLY FADES FOREVER

Queen Victoria, Queen of the United Kingdom of Great Britain and Ireland and the first Empress of India, is dead. Her son will be pleased. Old Vic has ruled for a total of 63 years, seven months and two days – the longest reign in British history.

As she had wished, her own sons lifted her into the coffin. Not the sort of job most people would like, but the new King Edward VII has waited a long time to get his bottom on the throne. He won't have minded popping his mum into the wide wooden box.

The dead queen was dressed in a white dress and her wedding veil – the sad old woman was going to meet her husband, Prince Albert, in heaven. She was buried beside Albert and her years of misery are at an end.

### BRIGHT START
She started off brightly enough. She was just 18 when she took the throne and just 20 when she married her cousin Albert. When Albert died 20 years later

she became the misery monarch. She dressed in black, had Albert's clothes laid out on his bed every day and went off to her palaces at Balmoral in Scotland or on the Isle of Wight.

## VICTORIA –
### THE INCREDIBLE SULK

She blamed her son Edward – she said his bad behaviour had killed hubby Albert. In fact, it was bad drains that had let sewage into Albert's drinking water.

The country just got along without her. Vic was hardly seen by the people – the people who suffered in slimy slums, choked in foul factories or starved in the streets. Vic got fat. Her own doctor said that when she took off her clothes she looked like a barrel.

### LOTS OF PEOPLE

Then an odd thing happened. There had been seven plots to kill Queen Vic. In 1887, when Vic had been on the throne 50 years, there was a great party planned in London. Vic had to appear. This was the chance for plot number eight to bump her off. The plotters wanted to blow her up in Westminster Abbey when she went for a church service. Vic escaped and the people decided she wasn't such a bad old stick after all. As the awful Scottish poet William Topaz McGonagall wrote:

> God prosper long our noble Queen,
> And long may she reign!
> Maclean he tried to shoot her,
> But it was all in vain.
>
> For God He turned the ball aside
> Maclean aimed at her head;
> And he felt very angry
> Because he didn't shoot her dead.

But, now she is dead, the Brit people are singing a happy song. Fat Vic has made way for fat Edward, and there will be lots of parties for the new king … at last. As the song says:

> *Father's going to change his socks*
> *and auntie take a bath*
> *On the day King Edward gets*
> *his crown on.*
> *With a brick we'll hit the teacher to*
> *make the kids all laugh,*
> *On the day King Edward gets*
> *his crown on.*
> *The lodger's going to get blind drunk*
> *as soon as day begins,*
> *Sister's wearing bloomers tied up*
> *with safety pins,*
> *To celebrate the great event, mother*
> *will have twins,*
> *On the day King Edward gets his*
> *crown on.*
> *So Victoria is dead at last. It's time*
> *to have a party!*

# RUTHLESS RULERS

**M**any rulers in history have been bad. Many have been mad. Some have been mad and bad. Here are a fearsome five.

## QIN SHI HUANGDI
## EMPEROR OF CHINA (259–210 BC)

Don't just plan to rule in this life. Why not be buried with an army of mud soldiers so you can rule in the next life, too?

## Claim to Fame

★ Qin Shi Huangdi was the first emperor of China. He was king of the Quin region then conquered the rest to make them into one.

★ His capital Xianyang had 270 small palaces. They were joined by secret passages and bridges. He moved secretly from one to the other to keep him safe from his enemies. No one was allowed to say which palace the emperor was in ... or they would die.

★ Qin Shi Huangdi was buried in a tomb 5 km wide. It is guarded by an 'army' of 8,000 soldiers and horses made from clay. They are known as the Terracotta Army and they were discovered in 1974.

## RUTHLESS RULER

Most warrior kings took prisoners in Chinese battles. Qin Shi Huangdi didn't. Enemy prisoners were all executed.

No one was allowed to argue with Qin Shi Huangdi. Four hundred and sixty writers wrote some unkind things about the emperor. They were buried with only their heads above ground. After starving for a few days the heads were lopped off.

HE'S SLICED IT!

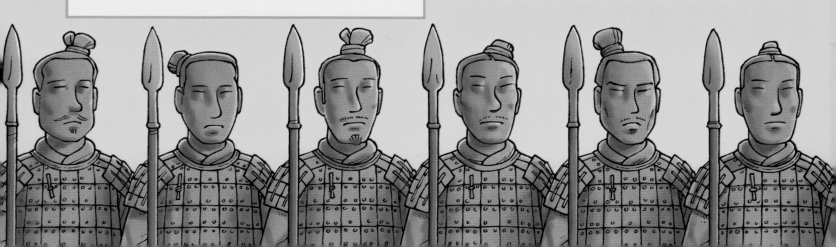

## FOUL FACT

QIN SHI HUANGDI DIED AND THE PRIME MINISTER, LI SI, WANTED TO KEEP IT A SECRET FOR A COUPLE OF WEEKS. THE EMPEROR'S CORPSE WAS PUT IN A CARRIAGE AND THEY SET OFF ON THE LONG TRIP TO THE CAPITAL. LI SI VISITED THE CARRIAGE EVERY DAY TO CHAT TO THE EMPEROR.
THEN LI SI GAVE ORDERS FOR TWO CARTS OF FISH TO BE DRIVEN IN FRONT OF THE EMPEROR'S CARRIAGE. WHY? BECAUSE THE FISH HAD A STRONG SMELL. NO ONE NOTICED THE OTHER SMELL – THE SMELL OF THE EMPEROR'S CORPSE GOING ROTTEN.

## FANTASTIC FACT

Qin Shi Huangdi was afraid of death. No one was even allowed to say the word 'death' in his palace. Then he heard a tale...

Hundreds of men and women set off on ships to search for the mountain. They were never seen in China again. Did they sink? No. They were too scared to go home without the drug. Qin Shi Huangdi would have had them executed.

## FUNNY FACT

Emperor Qin Shi Huangdi liked to tour the empire. That gave assassins lots of chances to kill him. He slept in a different room each night. He got servants to dress like him so an assassin wouldn't be sure who to kill. Emperor Qin Shi Huangdi didn't like men with weapons too close, so he said...

BUT, when assassin Jing Ke attacked the emperor with a poison dagger the guards weren't close enough to help. Qin Shi Huangdi ran for his life and raged...

How did Jing Ke get close to the emperor with a weapon? He said he had killed an enemy general. To prove it he carried the dead general's head into the palace ... probably dripping blood on the emperor's nice clean floors, so don't try this at school. The poison dagger was hidden inside a rolled-up map. Qin Shi Huangdi lived – Jing Ke was cut to pieces.

Qin Shi Huangdi's doctors made their own pills to keep him alive. Mercury pills. Too much mercury will kill you. Qin Shi Huangdi ate too many ... and died from the pills that were supposed to keep him alive.

# Queen Brunhilda of Austrasia
## North-east France (ad 543–613)

Even grannies can be ruthless rulers…

## Claim to Fame

★ Brunhilda said she was ruling for her sons and grandsons and even her great-grandsons … but she was really ruling for herself. She grew famous for being cruel and greedy.

★ When her first husband was murdered she married her nephew. What did he call her? Aunty? Wife? It caused a lot of trouble so she ordered his servant to kill him. End of problem.

★ She was blamed for the murder of ten other kings, bumped off to keep her family in power.

## RUTHLESS RULER

Brunhilda had two grandsons, Theodoric and Theodebert. She liked young Theodoric and wanted him to be the next king. Brunhilda wasn't so keen on Theodebert … grandparents can be funny like that. Granny Brunhilda said…

SORRY, THEODORIC, BUT YOU'LL JUST HAVE TO MURDER YOUR BROTHER IF YOU WANT THE THRONE

IF YOU SAY SO, GRANNY

GRANNY KNOWS BEST

Would you murder your brother just because your Gran tells you to? Theodoric did. Yes, grandparents can be funny … but they aren't usually THAT funny.

Anyway, it was a waste of time. Killer Theodoric died of the disease dysentery the next year and Brunhilda tried to get her great-grandson on to the throne. The young boy was *throne* off by the nobles. He was executed with Brunhilda.

### FOUL FACT

BRUNHILDA MARRIED SIGBERT. SIGBERT'S BROTHER, CHILPERIC, WAS JEALOUS SO HE MARRIED BRUNHILDA'S SISTER. BUT HE GOT BORED AND FOUND A NEW GIRLFRIEND, FREDEGUND. CHILPERIC AND FREDEGUND HAD BRUNHILDA'S SISTER MURDERED. SHE WAS STRANGLED IN HER SLEEP.

EASIER THAN A DIVORCE

SAYS WHO?

BRUNHILDA WAS CROSS AND ORDERED HER HUSBAND TO GO TO WAR WITH HIS BRUTAL BROTHER AND GORY GIRLFRIEND. BRUNHILDA LOST AND HUBBY SIGBERT WAS MURDERED.

## FANTASTIC FACT

Brunhilda's first husband, Sigbert, was murdered horribly in AD 575. His brother, Chilperic, sent two young assassins to kill him. The young men said they needed to talk to the king. When they were close enough they each drew a dagger. They stabbed him, one in each side. Both daggers were poisoned. Nasty.

Brunhilda got her own back. She had Chilperic assassinated. One bad turn deserves another, as they say.

## FUNNY FACT

Brunhilda came to a messy end. She was captured by her enemies along with her four great-grandsons. Two of the boys were killed on the spot. The two younger ones had their hair cut off and were sent to be monks.

They were lucky. Brunhilda would have a more painful end. First she was tortured on a rack for three days. A report said...

Then the army of France and Burgundy joined into one. They all shouted together that death would be the best thing for the evil Brunhilda. Then King Clotaire ordered that she be lifted on to a camel and led through the entire army. They pelted her with mud.

Brunhilda was tied by the hair, the hands and feet to wild horses and torn limb from limb. Finally she died. Her last grave was the fire. Her bones were burnt.

She was nearly 70 years old when she was torn apart. She was probably falling apart anyway.

# RICHARD III
## KING OF ENGLAND (1452–1485)

Some leaders will kill anyone who's a threat to them … even poor little kids.

## Claim to Fame

★ Richard took the crown from his nephew, Edward V, and probably murdered him along with Ed's little bruv Richard. The boys were aged about 12 and 10 when they 'disappeared' in the Tower of London.

★ Richard's older brother, the Duke of Clarence, was a traitor. He was sent to the Tower to be executed. It was said that he was drowned in a barrel of Malmsey wine … and Richard was the killer who pushed him in.

★ Richard is either loved or hated by many people. Some say he was a heroic soldier and a strong leader. Others say he was a villain who had an ugly and twisted body. Nobody can agree.

HEROIC, STRONG AND LET'S NOT FORGET ABOUT DROP DEAD GORGEOUS

## RUTHLESS RULER

Richard III had his friend Lord Hastings executed. Richard made up an excuse to quarrel with Hastings then said…

I WILL NOT EAT MY SUPPER TONIGHT UNTIL YOUR HEAD IS OFF YOUR SHOULDERS

GULP!

Guards rushed in and dragged Hastings out. They didn't have a block handy so they borrowed a piece of wood from a carpenter who'd been doing some repairs. They laid his neck on it and lopped his head off.

The Tower of London has some low doorways. What did they say to Hastings as they led him out?

MIND YOUR HEAD, SIR!

FUN-NEE

Richard enjoyed his supper. Hastings didn't.

## FOUL FACT

RICHARD III WAS THE LAST ENGLISH KING TO DIE ON THE BATTLEFIELD. HE WORE HIS CROWN SO HIS MEN KNEW WHO TO FOLLOW, BUT HIS ENEMIES COULD ALSO SEE WHO TO KILL! RICHARD CHARGED STRAIGHT DOWN THE HILL TOWARDS ENEMY LEADER HENRY TUDOR, AND CUT DOWN THE TUDOR FLAG – BY HACKING THE ARM OFF THE MAN HOLDING IT. RICHARD NEVER REACHED HENRY. HIS HORSE WAS BROUGHT DOWN AND HE WAS CHOPPED TO BITS BY HENRY'S SOLDIERS. RICHARD WAS KILLED IN THE LAST GREAT CHARGE OF KNIGHTS IN ARMOUR IN BRITAIN.
THE STORY THAT RICHARD'S CROWN WAS FOUND HANGING ON A THORN BUSH, AND WAS HANDED TO HENRY, IS PROBABLY UNTRUE.

## FUNNY FACT

Richard III's life was shown in a play by William Shakespeare. Richard is shown as an ugly hunchback with an evil history. Some people think this is terribly unfair. They say Richard was a strong but fair ruler and Shakespeare had it all wrong. They formed The Richard III Society. Richard is probably the only king of England to have his own fan club.

## FANTASTIC FACT

Richard was buried in a secret grave. His stone coffin was paid for by Henry Tudor, who went on to become King Henry VII.

There is a story that the coffin became a horse trough for many years. Later it was broken up to make steps for a pub cellar.

Henry Tudor stinks

RICHARD RICHARD GO, GO, GO!

WE ♥ R III

# Don Carlos
## Prince of Spain (1545–1568)

If you are a prince you can't trust anyone — not even your dear old dad.

## Claim to Fame

★ Don Carlos was a sad and sickly child. He grew up hunchbacked and pigeon-breasted, with shoulders of uneven height and his right leg a lot shorter than the left. He spoke in a high, girly voice and stuttered badly. His dad, King Philip, was worried that one day dull Don would become king.

★ Philip of Spain was a ruthless ruler but his son, Prince Don Carlos, was far more cruel and evil. Philip thought it would be a disaster for Spain if Don Carlos ever took the throne. He had his son locked away. Then one day in 1568 Prince Carlos died. How? His death is a history mystery.

★ In his cell Don Carlos went on hunger strikes and was force-fed with soup. Then he started swallowing things — even a diamond ring.

## RUTHLESS RULER

Before he was five years old, deadly Don started biting serving girls. Three nearly died from his attacks.

By the age of nine he was torturing little girls and animals for fun.

Don liked roasting small animals alive (but not little girls — he liked to whip them). He enjoyed roasting live hares best — a hare-raising hobby.

Prince Don once bit the head off a snake. Maybe he fancied a snake-snack? He was a greedy eater.

He once carved up a stable-full of horses so badly that 20 had to be put down.

HE'S BEEN EATING JEWELLERY

AND HIS DEATH IS A MYSTERY?

SNAKE BITE!

## FOUL FACT

**DON WAS CHASING A GIRL WHEN HE FELL DOWNSTAIRS AND GASHED HIS HEAD. HIS HEAD SWELLED UP. NO ONE COULD CURE HIM. SO PRIESTS TOOK THE MUMMY OF OLD SAINT DIEGO, WHO HAD BEEN DEAD 100 YEARS, AND POPPED IT INTO BED WITH DON.**

COULDN'T I HAVE A TEDDY?

**WOULD YOU BELIEVE IT? DON GOT BETTER! WELL, HIS WOUND GOT BETTER BUT HE GREW MORE AND MORE MAD, HAD VIOLENT RAGES AND ATTACKED PEOPLE. HE TRIED TO THROW A SERVANT OUT OF A TOWER WINDOW. HE MADE A SHOE-MAKER CUT UP A PAIR OF BOOTS AND EAT THEM.**
**HE TOLD A PRIEST HE WANTED TO 'KILL A MAN' ... AND IT WAS CLEAR THE MAN HE WANTED TO KILL WAS HIS OWN DAD, KING PHILIP. SOMETHING HAD TO BE DONE ABOUT DREADFUL DON. SO HE WAS LOCKED IN THE TOWER OF ARÉVALO CASTLE.**

## FANTASTIC FACT

*There were all sorts of stories about how Don Carlos died – some say poison, some say he was smothered, others that he was beheaded or he was simply left to starve to death.*

*The Horrible Histories answer?*

*Don Carlos had a fever and was sick non-stop. He poured ice water on the floor of his prison so that he could lie naked in it. Snow was brought in great barrels to cool him. For days he ate only fruit. Then he asked for a pie. A huge spicy pie was made for him and he ate it all. He washed it down with more than 10 litres of ice water. His sickness grew worse. When a priest came to pray for him Don threw up over the priest.*

*He died soon after. Murder?*

*King Philip gave his son everything he wanted in his prison. But the greedy prince stuffed himself with partridge livers washed down with iced water. This gave him a chill and he died. Not murdered ... but dead of his own greed.*

## FUNNY FACT

When Don Carlos was born, his great-grandmother was still alive, but locked away. She was known as Juana the Mad. She had fallen in love with Philip the Handsome of Austria and married him. When Philip died, Juana went mad with misery. After five weeks she heard a tale that her husband's corpse had been stolen. She had the coffin opened ... and threw herself on to the corpse, kissing the feet.

Juana travelled round Spain with her husband's coffin. Every now and then she would open it to check on the mouldering man inside. Finally she was locked away in a tower with nothing to eat but bread and cheese. She died after 50 years.

That was Don Carlos's great-grandmother.

# NAPOLEON BONAPARTE
## EMPEROR OF FRANCE (1769–1821)

Even great leaders have some funny — and disgusting — tales to tell.

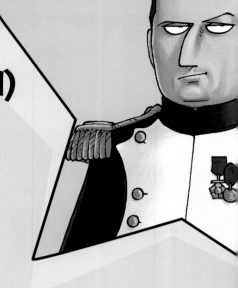

## Claim to Fame

★ Napoleon was a little bloke from Corsica. He came to France when it was being attacked by the rest of Europe. He led the French army in 20 years of war and almost beat the lot.

★ Napoleon was such a great fighter that the French made him emperor of the country. In the end he was defeated and fled from Paris in disguise. He gave his guide a tip – a banknote. But the note had a picture of Napoleon on it, of course. The guide handed him over to the British enemy.

★ Napoleon was captured and made prisoner on the island of Elba (in the Mediterranean Sea). But he escaped and started the wars all over again. In the end he was beaten at the Battle of Waterloo. This time he was packed off to a tiny island in the Atlantic Ocean. No escape.

POO BUMZ

## RUTHLESS RULER

One of Napoleon's first jobs was to fight for the French government AGAINST the French people. There were riots in Paris in 1795. Napoleon grabbed a few cannons and loaded them with grapeshot. Grapeshot is a bag of metal pellets. When they are fired at people they spread out and shred skin, put out eyes and snap off arms and legs.

The rioters had sticks and stones. Napoleon turned his grapeshot cannon on them. End of riot ... except for picking up bits of rioters that had been blown off.

This ruthless massacre made Napoleon rich and famous.

Napoleon's armies went as far as Africa, but he was sending them into danger ... and not just from their enemies. In 1799, Napoleon's troops marched through the desert on the way to Syria. They made a horrible mistake – they stopped for a drink at some dirty water full of bloodsucking leeches. The leeches stuck themselves to the insides of the soldiers' noses and throats. Hundreds of soldiers died of blood loss or choked to death.

## FOUL FACT #

In 1800 plotters set out to kill Napoleon. They loaded a barrel of gunpowder on to a cart and drove it to where Napoleon was driving past. The cart driver lit the fuse then handed the reins of the old horse to a girl. Napoleon lived. The girl was blown to pieces. How did Napoleon's police find the cart driver?

They took the remains of the dead horse to Paris horse-sellers and found out who had bought it. Four plotters went to the guillotine and had their heads sliced off.

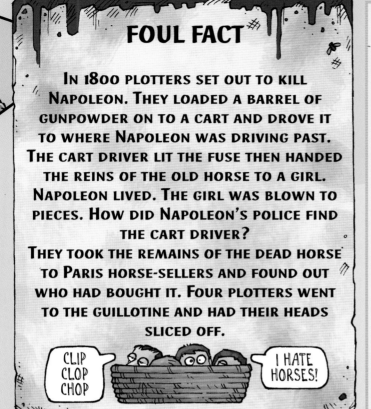

CLIP CLOP CHOP

I HATE HORSES!

## FUNNY FACT

General Berthier set up a great shooting party for Napoleon. The night before, he filled his park with rabbits so there were lots of bunnies to blast.

The trouble is they were tame rabbits. They were fed twice a day. When Napoleon set out to hunt them, the rabbits mistook him for their keeper. They charged at him, looking for their dinner. Napoleon had to run away to his carriage as hundreds of rabbits raced round him.

## FANTASTIC FACT

Napoleon is famous for being madly in love with his first wife, Josephine. But at the time they married, Josephine had few teeth left and they were mostly black. She wore heavy make-up to hide the dark circles under her eyes.

Still, Napoleon was crazy about his new bride. 'I love her to the point of madness and I cannot be apart from her,' he once said. Another time he said that she had the finest bottom he had ever seen.

We don't know if Josephine felt the same about him. He suffered from scabies so his face was often covered with foul-smelling sores. Josephine's dog didn't like him. When Napoleon went to cuddle her the dog jumped up and bit him!

He had several other illnesses. He had colic, which made him doze off in the middle of a battle. He had piles – an awful pain in the bum – which meant he could not always sit on a horse. At Waterloo he left the battlefield because of illness and THAT'S what lost him the war.

# ROTTEN REBELS

Someone has to stand up to those monstrous monarchs. Someone has to rebel. The trouble is, it can be a dangerous and deadly job.

## SPARTACUS (120–71 BC)

Spartacus was a gladiator and slave who rose up against the Romans. He vanished, but his followers were horribly punished…

### HORRIBLE HIGHLIGHTS

Spartacus the gladiator taught young gladiators. But he wanted to go home to Thrace (Bulgaria) and plotted an escape. Gladiators practised with wooden swords – they weren't allowed to use real swords until they went into the arena. So how did they make their escape past the Roman soldiers guarding them?

a) They went to the gladiator kitchens and pinched the knives.

b) They made their wooden swords really sharp and splintered the guards to death.

c) They put poison on the tips of their wooden swords and stabbed the guards.

ANSWER: (a) Spartacus armed his pupils with knives from the kitchens and led a rebellion. Once they'd cut a few Roman soldier throats, of course, they could then steal the Roman weapons.

# SPARTACUS — THE GORY DETAILS

❋ The young gladiators overpowered their guards, stole their weapons and escaped. They made camp on the slopes of the volcano Mount Vesuvius.

❋ Sadly the rebel slaves decided they didn't want to go home. They forced Spartacus to turn back and attack Rome. The slave army could not defeat the might of the Roman Empire. Roman General Crassus defeated the rebels.

❋ As a lesson to all slaves, 6,000 rebels were crucified by the side of the road to Rome. Crassus did not give orders for the bodies to be taken down. Slaves walking along the road were forced to see the bodies for years after the last battle. It was a warning. No one knows if Spartacus was killed in the final battle or if he was caught alive and executed.

# AL-KAHINA — QUEEN OF THE BERBERS (DIED AD 690s)

A good rebel leader can see into the future. Maybe.

## HORRIBLE HIGHLIGHTS

Al-Kahina was this North African rebel's nickname - it meant 'fortune teller'. Her enemies thought she could see into the future. Useful. Al-Kahina's tribe were prisoners of a cruel warrior chief. How did she set them free?

a) She set fire to his palace and turned him into a crisp.

b) She married him then murdered him in bed.

c) She dug a tunnel and they all ran away.

ANSWER: b) The warrior chief was always guarded. Al-Kahina married him then said, 'Time for bed, hubby dear'. When he took off his armour she picked up his sword and gave him the chop. That's what you call a horrible honeymoon.

# Al-Kahina — The Gory Details

🟣 Al-Kahina and her travelling Berber people defeated an army of Arabs. To stop them returning for revenge she wrecked the towns of her own people – the town Berbers. She burned their orchards and killed their animals. She said, 'They want our gold and silver. Let's burn down our towns and bury our riches in ashes.' That just made her town Berbers angry. Big mistake.

🟣 The avenging Arabs returned and captured her. But she was supposed to be a fortune teller. Why didn't she see that coming?

🟣 The Arabs said, 'You are a woman, so we won't kill you. Just promise to stop this rebellion … and get your people to pay us!' Al-Kahina refused. Then, just to spite them, she took poison and died. (Or maybe she was executed. Or maybe she was killed in battle. It was a l-o-n-g time ago.)

> I DON'T SUPPOSE THERE'S ANY CHANCE I DIED OF OLD AGE?

# Philippe van Artevelde – French rebel leader (about 1340–1382)

Lords invented taxes. Poor people hated paying them. So history has always had tax rebels who fought and died to hang on to their cash…

## HORRIBLE HIGHLIGHTS
In France in the Middle Ages the lords raised taxes and often used the money to pay for their own fun. In 1379 lords charged peasants a tax for what?

a) A new swimming pool for a castle in Calais

b) A birthday party for the Countess of Nantes

c) A tournament for knights to have pretend battles

ANSWER: c) Tax collectors went into houses to check what food people had and made them pay tax on it. The people were furious – as you would be if someone marched in and stuck their nose in YOUR fridge. The people refused to pay. They rioted and the riots spread through France. Reports said the poor ATE the rich. A witness said: 'They cut open the bodies and ate the flesh of Christian men as if they were animals.' The revolt was crushed cruelly. Rebels were hanged and their children sold as slaves.

# PHILIPPE – THE GORY DETAILS

✸ The peasants had short memories and were revolting again just three years later. The rebels started by stealing 3,000 'Maillotins' – or mallets – for weapons. These lead hammers on sticks were pretty deadly if you smashed someone with one. (And very painful if you dropped one on your toe.) The rebels became known as 'Maillotins', even when they weren't carrying heavy hammers.

✸ In the south of France, 40 of the rebels had a get-rich-quick idea. First you find all the men with more than 100 pounds. Next, you kill them. Then, you marry their widows and get their money. There was just one little problem – most of the 40 rebels already had a wife. How did they plan to solve that? They decided to murder their own wives first so they'd be free to marry the rich widows. Nice people.

✸ The northern rebels were smashed at a battle near Roosebeke. The young King Charles VI asked to see the rebel leader, Artevelde, dead or alive. He was dead. The young king bravely walked up to Artevelde's corpse and gave it a good kicking. The body was then taken away and hanged from a tree. (Don't worry, it didn't hurt a bit.) But the Duke of Burgundy had a nastier little bit of revenge. He had a tapestry woven and the tapestry showed the face of Artevelde. The duke then used the tapestry as a carpet so he was able to trample over Artevelde's face whenever he felt like it.

TAKE ZAT!

LE THUMP

# Charles-Henri Sanson – French executioner (1739-1806)

Rebel leaders can order executions. But someone has to do the bloody job. Some rebel executioners even get to like it.

## HORRIBLE HIGHLIGHTS

The French people formed their own government in 1789 - The Assembly - and started telling King Louis XVI what to do. He was a good boy - for a year or so. Then Louis made a b-i-g mistake that would cost him his life. What did he do?

a) He refused to bow down in front of the rebel leader, Danton.

b) He tried to escape from France to get help from other kings.

c) He got into a fight with one of his guards and killed him.

ANSWER: b) The queen and the princes disguised themselves and set off in a coach. King Louis dressed in a large dark wig and a round hat. He left in a separate coach. The royal family was spotted and arrested before they reached the border. The journey back to Paris was grim. The peasants had really turned against the royal family now. They spat at the king and tore the queen's clothes. Furious gangs jumped on the carriage, and wild women swore at the royal family.

# Charles-Henri – the gory details

🌸 Rebel leader Marat said, 'Let the blood of the traitors flow. It is the only way to save France.' Blood of the posh people was top of the list, of course. To kill the posh people painlessly the guillotine had been invented. And the ace executioner was Charles-Henri Sanson. Louis XVI was executed in January 1793. He died horribly. He was laid face-down on the guillotine and the executioner, Sanson, pulled the rope. The blade fell. The king screamed. His neck was so fat that the blade failed to slice through it first time. It came off at the second attempt.

✸ A young guard, about 18 years old, picked up the head for the crowd to see. 'Long live the Revolution!' they cried. They rushed forward to dip handkerchiefs in the blood. The inventor of the machine was Dr Joseph-Ignace Guillotin. He said, 'The blade falls like lightning; the head flies off; the blood spurts; the man no longer exists.' He told the Revolution leaders, 'Gentlemen, with my machine, I'll take off your head in a flash, and you won't even feel the slightest pain.' They tested it on corpses. (Did they buy them at the local chopping centre?)

✸ Charles-Henri Sanson was good at his job and once executed 300 men and women in three days. But he wasn't keen on executing women and he did not enjoy executing King Louis XVI – but he didn't dare refuse. It was a tricky job, high up on the blood-soaked platform. One day Charles-Henri's son, Gabriel, was helping dad to dead-head the traitors. Gabriel slipped, fell off the platform and crashed to the cobbled street below. Gabriel died. After that a fence was put up round the guillotine platform.

✸ In 1793 and 1794 between 20,000 and 40,000 people lost their lives under the blade of the guillotine. They called this time 'The Reign of Terror'. The Sanson family kept the job for the next 50 years.

WATCH THAT EDGE, SON, IT'S A DEATH TRAP

# VLADIMIR ILYICH LENIN (1870–1924)

Sometimes rebels just set out to get revenge for their dead friends and family – but the revenge can be sheer murder.

## HORRIBLE HIGHLIGHTS

Vladimir Ilyich Ulyanov became known as Lenin - the leader of the Russian Revolution. When he was born Russia was ruled by emperors known as tsars. Some of these tsars were mad, some bad and some quite good. But Lenin decided they had to go. Why?

a) The tsar's men had kicked Lenin's dog when they called to collect his taxes.

b) The tsar's men had thrown Lenin's mother in a freezing river because she smelled awful and needed a bath.

c) The tsar's men had hanged Lenin's brother.

ANSWER: c) Lenin's older brother, Alexander, was arrested for plotting to blow up the tsar, who was also called Alexander. They hanged Alexander (not the tsar) and he didn't do a lot of plotting after that. Alexander (not the bomb plotter) died seven years later and Lenin would take a terrible revenge on his son, Tsar Nicholas II, and all his family.

# LENIN – THE GORY DETAILS

❀ Lenin started to plot a revolution and was sent away to the frozen region of Siberia to a prison camp (to cool off a bit, I suppose). He met other rebels there, of course, so prison did him no good at all. When he was set free he travelled around Europe and went to other rebel cities … like Manchester.

The First World War started in 1914 and it was the best thing that ever happened to Lenin. The Russian people were battered and starved by the war. Who could they blame? The tsar. Who would lead a rebellion? Lenin! Lenin stuck a wig on his bald head and shaved off his beard so he could sneak back into Russia. In October 1917 Lenin's rebels attacked the Winter Palace in St Petersburg. They threw out the government and took over. The tsar and his family were sent to a house out of the way. Six months later they were taken to the cellar and everyone, even the children and servants, was shot dead.

Lenin set up the Secret Police to execute anyone who got in his way. So, of course, there were lots of plots to kill him. In 1918 he was shot.

He lived, but the wounds left him weak and one bullet stayed in his neck. He died six years later – so it was a s-l-o-w sort of death by bullet. The French Revolution had their 'Reign of Terror' – Lenin had his 'Red Terror', with bullets instead of guillotines. Some say 280,000 died. It made the French 'Reign of Terror' look like a 'Reign of a-bit-of-a-fright'. As for the next Russian leader, Joseph Stalin, as many as 60 MILLION died in the Terrors. Lenin was just a beginner.

HE'S JUST A HORRIBLE MASS-MURDERER – BUT I'M A TRULY HIDEOUS MALEVOLENT MONSTER

LENIN? EVIL TYRANT? HE'S JUST AN AMATEUR

# POTTY PRIESTS

**R**eligion has caused more death and misery than anything else in history. People say, 'My God's better than your God,' or even, 'I am your God!'

## AMENHOTEP IV – EGYPTIAN KING

### ALSO KNOWN AS AKHENATEN (ABOUT 1353 BC–1336 BC)

Egyptian kings liked to think they died and joined the other gods in heaven. Amenhotep couldn't wait. He said he was a god on Earth – Akhenaten.

His mummy has never been found … so maybe it's a mangled and mashed mummy, as they say.

# POPE JOHN XII (AD 937–964)

Religious jobs give you power – some people enjoy the power and forget about the religion.

The devil is not daft enough to damage a potty, no-pray pope like that. It had to be the hubby to blame.

# ATAHUALPA – INCA EMPEROR (1502–1533)

Some leaders are daft enough to die for their religion.

As far as we know, Atahualpa is still looking for a body. So guard yours with your life.

# OLIVER CROMWELL (1599-1658)
## LORD PROTECTOR OF ENGLAND FROM 1653-1658

Some religious men will kill you to save your soul. They are God's warriors.

CROMWELL WAS A PURITAN CHRISTIAN. HE WAS PART OF THE GOVERNMENT THAT RULED IN A VERY STRICT WAY. THEY EVEN BANNED CHRISTMAS

CROMWELL WAS STRICT WITH HIS OWN TROOPS. HE HAD TWO MEN HANGED FOR STEALING HENS FROM AN IRISH PEASANT WOMAN

BOB EDWARDS / ROUNDHEAD

**HH NATIONAL NEWS**

CROMWELL AND HIS FRIENDS HAD KING CHARLES I BEHEADED BECAUSE THEY SQUABBLED ABOUT WAR AND RELIGION

I KNEW I'D MAKE HEADLINES ONE DAY

HILARIOUS, YOUR MAJESTY

CHARLES I          KING

**HHNN**

PRIESTS IN WEXFORD, IRELAND, WERE FLOGGED TO DEATH, THEN THEIR BODIES WERE FLUNG INTO DRAINS

SOLDIERS OFTEN DRESSED IN CATHOLIC PRIESTS' CLOTHES TO MAKE FUN OF THEIR VICTIMS, THOUGH IT WAS SAID THAT THEY TURNED SICK AND DIED SOON AFTER!

OO-ER

TWO YEARS AFTER HIS DEATH, CROMWELL'S BODY WAS DUG UP, CUT UP AND THROWN IN THE RIVER THAMES

AND HIS HEAD WAS STUCK ON A POLE AT WESTMINSTER HALL FOR 25 YEARS. THAT'S OLIVER – TOP ROUND HEAD

I CAN'T SEE THE POINT

**HHNN**

Cromwell died in 1658. The English invited chopped Charlie's son, Charles II, to take his dad's throne. So was it worth it, Ollie?

# HONG XIUQUAN – CHINESE EMPEROR (1814–1864)

Some religious rulers just don't know when to stop being cruel. They carry on even after they die.

HONG XIUQUAN CALLED HIMSELF THE HEAVENLY KING. IF YOU FORGOT TO CALL HIM 'HEAVENLY', YOU WERE EXECUTED

WHY NOT? I'M A HEAVENLY MAN, BABE

OF COURSE, HE HAD HEAVENLY POWERS. WHEN HIS PEOPLE STARVED, HE SAID...

EAT SWEET DEW

WHEN HIS STARVED PEOPLE WERE DEFEATED, HONG XIUQUAN DECIDED TO TAKE POISON

ORDINARY POISON ISN'T GOOD ENOUGH FOR A HEAVENLY KING, SO I SWALLOWED GOLD LEAF

HE DIED, BUT HIS CRUELTY WENT ON. THE GARDEN OF THE HEAVENLY KING HAD TREES ... AND FROM EVERY TREE THERE DANGLED ONE OF HONG XIUQUAN'S MANY WIVES

NO NOOSE IS GOOD NEWS

The Heavenly King may have been happy in heaven, but what about those rope-choked wives?

# WICKED WOMEN

L ots of men in history are horrible. But women are forgotten. They can be just as horrible.

## BOUDICA – QUEEN OF THE ICENI (DIED AD 61)

If you are a woman and you are bullied then you survive by being a bigger and nastier bully.

### THE ROME OFFICE

## ROTTEN REPORT

**CRUEL CRIMES:** When Boudica rebelled against the Roman invaders, some of her prisoners were hung up naked. Roman women had their breasts cut off and sewed to their mouths, so it looked as if they were eating them. Afterwards they were impaled – a sharp pole was run through their bodies.

Boudica was forced to pay the Roman invaders. She had no money so they stripped her and beat her. When the Romans beat her in battle she took poison. Some say her grave today is under platform 8 of King's Cross station in London.

**WHAT THEY SAY:** Roman Dio Cassius said, *'She was huge and terrifying with a harsh voice. A great mass of bright red hair fell to her knees: she wore a twisted necklace, and a tunic of many colours, over which was a thick cloak, fastened by a brooch. Now she grasped a spear, to strike fear into all who watched her.'*

If big, bad Boud was alive today she'd make a great head teacher. No messing about in her school.

> IF YOUR HOMEWORK IS LATE AGAIN YOU WILL GET A DETENTION AND A LETTER HOME TO YOUR PARENTS – THEN I WILL HAVE YOU KILLED

# QUEEN GRUOCH OF SCOTLAND
## ALSO KNOWN AS LADY MACBETH (AD 994–1057)

Men ruled the world in past times. So, if you are a woman, you need to rule the men. Marry them if you have to.

Dunsinane Department of Justice

## ROTTEN REPORT

**CRUEL CRIMES:** Gruoch's husband was burned to death by Lord Macbeth. She married murdering Macbeth. As queen she was ruthless and cruel. She invited old King Duncan to stay at their castle … then had him stabbed to death in his bed. Macbeth became king and Gruoch his queen. But their evil caught up with them. Gruoch went mad and threw herself off the castle walls. Macbeth was caught in battle and beheaded.

Most of Gruoch's story was invented by William Shakespeare for his play, 'Macbeth'. Will Shakespeare made Macbeth out to be a villain who murdered old King Duncan. In fact he beat a young King Duncan in battle, fair and square. They say Gruoch burned her first husband to death so she was free to marry Macbeth and become queen. It's probably a lie.

**WHAT THEY SAY:** Shakespeare said Lady Macbeth wasn't bothered by the bloody body her husband had just murdered. She told him, *'Give me the daggers: the sleeping and the dead are but as pictures'*.

Someone should tell her the sleeping and the dead are NOT the same. Just ask bleeding Duncan when he fails to wake up.

YOU COULD SAY I'M DEAD TIRED

# ISABELLA OF FRANCE
## ALSO KNOWN AS THE SHE-WOLF OF FRANCE (1295–1358)

Women have been treated like animals in the past — married off as part of a deal between kings. But some could still fight back.

Palace Prosecution Bureau

# ROTTEN REPORT

**CRUEL CRIMES:** Isabella married the English king, Edward II, but then raised an army in France to fight him. Her boyfriend, Roger Mortimer, led the invasion of England. King Ed ran away to Wales and gave the throne to their son, Edward III. Ed II's friends were murdered - friends like the Bishop of Exeter, beheaded by a man with a butcher's knife. Isabella still wasn't happy. She had Ed II murdered at Berkeley Castle in 1327. They say the killers pushed a red-hot poker up his bum. Sizzle.

Isabella was just three years old when her dad said she would marry Edward II of England … but not till she grew up a little. Well, not till she was 12 years old anyway. She was beautiful but King Ed wasn't keen on her. He gave lots of wedding presents … to his best friend Piers Gaveston. When Ed II went to war with Scotland, he dumped Isabella at Tynemouth and she was left to escape the Scots. Mortimer was later hanged by Edward III. Isabella died peacefully and was buried in her wedding dress … along with the heart of Ed II.

**WHAT THEY SAY:** They say she sent the order to have Edward murdered. But she wrote a crafty letter in Latin, which said, *'Edwardum occidere nolite timere bonum est.'* Now that could mean: *'Do not be afraid to kill Edward; it is good.'* But Isabella would tell people it could also mean: *'Do not kill Edward; it is good to fear.'* Sneaky. The TRUTH is that the tale about the letter is a lie. (Some people said Isabella went mad after Mortimer was hanged. She didn't.)

I WASN'T MAD BUT I WAS QUITE CROSS

# Elizabeth Bathory 'The Blood Countess of Transylvania' (1560–1614)

Women are thought to be kind and caring. But some have been as cruel and bloodthirsty as any man. Really, really bloodthirsty.

*Transylvania Police Department*

## ROTTEN REPORT

CRUEL CRIMES: Bloody Bess was born in 1560 into one of the richest families in Transylvania. She should have had a happy life – but she killed over 600 women and girls in the early 1600s. Why? So she could have a bath in their blood. She thought it made her look young. Bloodthirsty Bess had horrible henchmen to help her. They drained the blood from the victims and filled the baths. But one of her victims escaped and told the law officers about what was happening at Castle Csejthe. On 30 December, 1610 they raided Castle Csejthe. They were horrified by the terrible sights there. In the dungeon they discovered several living girls, some of whose bodies had been half-drained of blood. Dead girls had been thrown to the wolves.

Bad Bess never went on trial and was never found guilty. Her henchmen were executed – beheaded and burned after having their fingers torn off – but Bess was simply put out of harm's way. Stonemasons were brought to Castle Csejthe to brick up the windows and doors of the bedroom with the countess inside. They left a small hole through which food could be passed. She stayed there for the rest of her life and died in the castle in 1614. BUT she tortured about 50 girls – not 600 – and the stories about baths in blood were made up later.

WHAT THEY SAY: Johannes Ujvary, Elizabeth's butler, said, *'About 37 girls have been killed. Six of them were taken to the castle by me. The victims were tied up and cut with scissors. Sometimes two witch friends of the countess tortured these girls. Sometimes the countess herself.'*

I NEED SOME NEW BLOOD AROUND HERE

# BELLE GUNNESS (1859–1931)

Some women have been driven by greed – driven to murder. And the more they get the more they want. 'Deadlier than the male,' they say…

## Indiana Sheriff's Office

# ROTTEN REPORT

**CRUEL CRIMES:** Belle killed most of her boyfriends, and her daughters, Myrtle and Lucy. Some say she killed over 100 people and got away with it. These people were insured – if they died then Belle got the money. Her houses burned down … and Belle got the insurance money. One husband died, probably of poison, but the next hubby, Peter Gunness, came to a weird end. Peter was working in a shed when part of a sausage-grinding machine fell from a high shelf, split his skull open and killed him on the spot. Belle advertised for boyfriends – they came to her farm, gave her their money – then vanished. No one knows how many she cuddled then killed and cut up and buried.

When she was 18 years old, sweet little Belle went to a dance. A man kicked her in the stomach. After that she turned cruel and ruthless. (The man died of stomach cancer soon after.) Belle's sister said, *'Belle was crazy for money. It was her great weakness.'* When the law began to suspect her, she faked her own death in a house fire. Her children were found dead along with the headless corpse of a woman. She had been poisoned. But it wasn't Belle. The killer queen was never seen again. She probably killed about 40 men, women and children.

**WHAT THEY SAY:** A folk song of the 1930s said:

> *'Belle wanted a husband, she wanted one bad,*
> *She placed in the papers a lonely-hearts ad.*
> *Men came to Belle Gunness to share food and bed,*
> *Not knowing that soon they'd be knocked in the head.'*

I'M NOT SURE WHAT'S WORSE – MULTIPLE MURDER OR THAT SONG

# Kruel for Killers

There are many famous murderers in history. But some of the most famous are innocent ... or are they?

## Iollas (Greek, died around 325 bc)  Victim: Alexander the Great

If a great leader dies suddenly then blame someone close to him...

ALEXANDER THE GREAT WAS ... WELL ... GREAT. HE CONQUERED THE WORLD AND MADE LOTS OF ENEMIES, OF COURSE. I WAS HIS CUP-BEARER - IMPORTANT JOB.

MY FRIEND, MEDIUS, HAD A FEAST FOR ALEXANDER WHERE MY BOSS DRANK HIMSELF TO DEATH. HE WAS ONLY 32.

MY BIT

FOR HE'S A JOLLY GREAT FEL-LOW! FOR HE'S A JOLL GRE

WHAT DO YOU KNOW? I GOT THE BLAME. THEY SAID I POISONED HIM. SLIPPED SOMETHING INTO HIS WINE! ME?!

THEY SAY I SMUGGLED THE POISON INTO BABYLON, HIDDEN IN THE HOOF OF A MULE. WHAT ASS SAID THAT?

ANYWAY, I DIED SOON AFTER, SO IT WAS EASY TO BLAME ME. BUT DID ALEX'S FRIENDS HAVE TO DIG ME UP AND CHOP UP MY CORPSE? IT'S NO FUN BEING DEAD.

I'M PRETTY CUT UP ABOUT THIS

## ☠ Did you know...? ☠

We'll never know how Alexander the Great died. Did he drink himself to death? Did he die of sickness from the many wounds he got in battles? Or disease? He died 12 days after he fell ill at the feast of Medius. But the Greeks didn't have poisons that took 12 days to work.

IOLLAS IS INNOCENT MAYBE?

# IVAR THE BONELESS (VIKING, DIED AD 873)  VICTIM: KING AELLA

People like horror stories. But the stories aren't always true, even if the people in them really did exist.

IT ALL STARTED WITH KING AELLA OF NORTHUMBRIA IN ENGLAND. HE KILLED MY DAD. HIS MEN PUSHED HIM IN A PIT OF POISON SNAKES.

SO, THEY SAY ME AND MY BROTHERS CAPTURED AELLA AND TOOK A TERRIBLE REVENGE. FIRST WE TIED HIM TO A TREE...

...THEN WE CUT HIS RIBS AWAY FROM HIS BACKBONE. VERY PAINFUL THAT ... DON'T TRY IT AT HOME.

OUCH

REALLY OUCH

THEN WE RIPPED OUT HIS LUNGS AND SPREAD THEM OVER HIS BACK LIKE THE WINGS OF AN EAGLE.

REALLY REALLY DEAD

THIS WAS THE FAMOUS BLOOD EAGLE TORTURE OF THE VIKINGS AND IT TAUGHT AELLA A REAL LESSON! BUT WHY WOULD I GO TO ALL THAT BLEEDING TROUBLE?

REALLY REALLY OUCH

## ✖ DID YOU KNOW...? ✖

The Viking legends said Ivar the Boneless had no bones. That is plain daft. So, don't believe the Viking stories. The story of the Blood Eagle also appears in Viking stories. They are scary tales made to frighten the enemy.

IVAR THE BONELESS IS INNOCENT PERHAPS?

# RATTUS RATTUS (1340s)

## VICTIM: 75 MILLION HUMANS

History writers like to find something to blame for horrible events. Sometimes it's the wrong something.

BACK IN 1347, A TERRIBLE PLAGUE STARTED KILLING THOSE HORRIBLE HUMANS. SEVENTY-FIVE MILLION DIED. WHO GOT THE BLAME? ME. RATTUS RATTUS, THE BLACK RAT.

THEY CALLED IT THE BLACK DEATH. WHAT THEY SAID WAS THE PLAGUE WAS CARRIED BY ME AND MY MATES, THE BLACK RATS...

WELL IT WASN'T. IT WAS CARRIED BY THE ORIENTAL RAT FLEA. THE FLEAS BIT US RATS AND GAVE US THE PLAGUE.

WHEN A RAT DIED, THE FLEAS GOT HUNGRY. IF A HUMAN WAS HANDY THEY JUMPED ON TO THEM, BIT THEM AND GAVE THEM THE PLAGUE.

THEY GOT BIG PURPLE-BLACK SPOTS AND DIED HORRIBLY. SORRY AND ALL THAT, BUT US BLACK RATS DIED TOO!

## ☠ DID YOU KNOW…? ☠

Rattus rattus is right. Rats have always been blamed for causing the plague. Oh, yes, they CARRIED the fleas around. Blame them for that. But they didn't cause the plague. Poor little vermin died too. Black Death meant Black Rat Death.

# WILLIAM CORDER (1803–1828)  VICTIM: MARIA MARTEN

The most famous killers in history never get a fair trial. After they die they are hated forever, but do they deserve it?

*I WAS THE MOST FAMOUS MURDERER IN BRITAIN ... TILL JACK THE RIPPER CAME ALONG 60 YEARS AFTER I WAS HANGED.*

*I WAS FROM A POSH FAMILY IN SUFFOLK. I MET THE WICKED MARIA MARTEN – A MOLE-CATCHER'S DAUGHTER – AND WE HAD A BABY. VERY NAUGHTY – WE WEREN'T MARRIED.*

*MARIA STARTED BLACKMAILING ME. SHE SAID I HAD TO MARRY HER OR GO TO PRISON. MARRIAGE? TO HER? IT WOULD BE A SHAME AND A DISGRACE.*

*I TOLD HER WE'D RUN AWAY TOGETHER. SHE MUST MEET ME IN MY FAMILY'S RED BARN AT MIDNIGHT.*

*WHEN SHE ARRIVED, MY PISTOL WENT OFF AND SHOT HER. I BURIED HER. A YEAR LATER I WAS ARRESTED AND HANGED.*

## ✄ DID YOU KNOW…? ✄

Corder became famous when plays called 'Murder in the Red Barn' were shown all around Britain. They showed Corder as a villain who chatted up poor young Maria Marten then killed her when she had a baby. The TRUTH is that big Maria was older than weedy little Corder. She DID have a baby with Corder but it was her THIRD baby.

The story was a great drama because they said Maria's ghost appeared and told her family where to find the body. Corder said he just pointed a pistol at her to scare her. The strong woman snatched at it and the gun went off by accident. Corder was hanged clumsily a year later – he died very slowly.

# Dr Hawley Harvey Crippen (1862–1910)  Victim: Cora Turner

Some killers are famous for curious things. The case against them is forgotten.

 I MARRIED THE SINGER CORA TURNER AND MOVED FROM AMERICA TO ENGLAND. SHE WAS AN AWFULLY BOSSY WOMAN.

IN ENGLAND I FELL IN LOVE WITH YOUNG ETHEL LE NEVE, AND IN 1910 CORA VANISHED. I SAID SHE'D GONE BACK TO AMERICA.

ETHEL AND I TOOK A SHIP FOR CANADA.

CHUG CHUG

...AND TAKE OUT THE RUBBISH!

YES DEAR

LONDON POLICE SEARCHED MY HOUSE AND FOUND THE REMAINS OF A HUMAN BODY BURIED UNDER THE BRICK FLOOR OF THE BASEMENT.

CRIPES

THEY SENT A RADIO SIGNAL TO THE SHIP. I WAS THE FIRST CRIMINAL TO BE ARRESTED USING RADIO. THAT'S WHAT MADE ME SO FAMOUS.

DOCTOR BERNARD SPILSBURY SAID THE BODY WAS CORA'S AND SHE'D BEEN POISONED.

OF COURSE THEY HANGED ME. BUT DID I DO IT?

## ❧ Did you know…? ❧

The corpse in the cellar had no arms, legs or head – they were never found. The police said the missing bits had been put in a bath of acid and washed away. The head was popped into a handbag and thrown into the English Channel.

Ethel le Neve was found 'not guilty'. But did Crippen kill Cora?

Doctor Bernard Spilsbury was not the best doctor in Britain. He made lots of mistakes. Did he get the corpse in the cellar wrong?

In October 2007 another doctor said new tests showed the corpse was NOT Cora!

DOCTOR CRIPPEN IS INNOCENT
MAYBE?

# WILD WARRIORS

**I**f your job is to kill people then you have to be ruthless. But some warriors have been a bit more than that...

## ARMINIUS – GERMAN WARRIOR (18 BC–AD 19)

One German warrior was up against a mighty war machine. He needed to be ruthless and sneaky...

### FIGHTING FACTS

✹ Arminius was the leader of the Cherusci tribe in Germany. The Roman Army had conquered Germany so Arminius had to get sneaky if he wanted to fight back.

✹ Arminius pretended to be friendly with Roman General Varus. He said there were rebels in the Teutoburger Forest and Varus had to sort them out.

✹ Arminius said he'd guide Varus and show him the way. When the Romans were deep inside the gloomy forest, the Cherusci turned and attacked.

✹ The Romans were massacred. Roman women and children were sacrificed to Cherusci gods. The Cherusci sliced them open and strung their guts from the trees.

### ARMINIUS'S TOP WEAPON:
**JAVELIN** – thrown from Cherusci hiding among the trees.

## EL CID – SPANISH WARRIOR (1043–1099)

El Cid was such a great warrior that his army was lost without him when he died. But there are ways of getting around little problems like that.

### FIGHTING FACTS

✹ Rodrigo Díaz de Vivar was a knight from Castille in Spain. But his Arab enemies called him 'El Cid', which means 'Lord'.

✹ El Cid had books about war read out to his soldiers so they would fight like the warriors in the old tales. (A bit like watching a crime film before you go off pick-pocketing.)

✹ El Cid was the terror of the Arab armies. He surrounded their cities and starved them. At Valencia, people were forced to eat the city's horses, dogs, cats and mice.

✹ El Cid battled against armies with swords and spears, yet it was a loose arrow that finished him off. After El Cid died, his wife strapped his body to his horse and sent it back into battle. His soldiers, thinking that their leader was riding to fight beside them, felt brave again. The enemy ran away. El Cid won his final battle even after his death.

to El Cid

with love from the Moors

El Cid rode a **HORSE** called 'Stupid'. He could pick any horse he wanted. When he picked the white one his friend said, 'That's an awful horse. It's babieca ... stupid!' The name stuck.

# SIMON DE MONTFORT 5TH EARL OF LEICESTER (1170–1218)

Great warriors know that you can't just defeat people in battle and hope they'll behave. You have to make an example of them. A cruel example…

## FIGHTING FACTS

✠ In 1209 Cathar rebels were fighting the Catholic Church in France. Simon de Montfort was sent from England to sort them out. He pulled out the eyes of the Cathars he caught, and sliced off their noses and lips. One man was left with one eye. The one-eyed man was given the job of leading his blind mates to the next fortress as a warning: 'Mess with Simon and you'll never see (or smell) your feet again.'

✠ Simon de M's excuse for the cruelty was that the Cathars had done the same to two Catholic knights. Other knights had their skin ripped off while they were alive, and ordinary soldiers often had hands or feet chopped off – if they were lucky. If they were unlucky they were simply chopped into pieces.

✠ Simon de Montfort moved on to Minerve in June 1210 and captured lots of Cathars. One hundred and forty of them refused to become Catholics. Sizzling Simon burned them on one big bonfire. Some witnesses said the Cathars were so happy to die that the Catholics didn't have to throw them on the bonfire – they threw themselves on. They were the toast of the town.

✠ The Lady of Lavaur sheltered 400 Cathars and refused to give them up to de Montfort. When she was captured in May 1211, Simon had her thrown down a well and stones piled on top of her. The lady died horribly, but not as horribly as some of her knights. Eighty of them were lined up to be hanged all at once. But the weight was too great and the hanging beam collapsed. They had their throats cut instead.

✠ **The women of a Cathar city used a war catapult to fire a boulder that crushed Simon's skull. Revenge!**

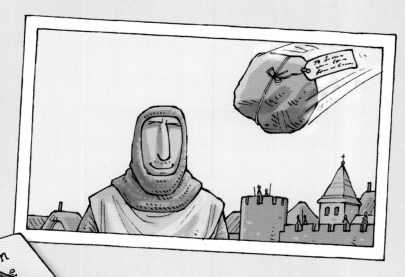

## SIMON DE MONTFORT'S TOP WEAPON:
**MANGONEL** – a war catapult useful for crushing skulls.

# VICE-ADMIRAL HORATIO NELSON (1758–1805)

People love heroes. But even great heroes have nasty little secrets their followers try to forget.

## FIGHTING FACTS

✖ Nelson was one of Britain's most famous sailors – he won the Battle of Trafalgar in 1805. Yet he was usually seasick when he went to sea. Pity the poor sailors that had to mop up after him. When he started in the Navy he was just 12 years old so he probably had to mop up his own sick.

✖ He won battles at sea, but lost an eye and an arm when he fought on land. (Of course, to make up for that, he lost his life at sea). He was a tough little bloke. When he was wounded in the arm at Santa Cruz he said, 'Tell the surgeon to hurry. I know I must lose my right arm, so the sooner it's off the better.' He was right. He was also right when he was shot at

the Battle of Trafalgar and said, 'It is nonsense, Mr Burke, to think I can live. My sufferings are great but they will soon be over.'

✖ Nelson may have been armless but he wasn't harmless. His sailors were flogged if they didn't do as they were told. Between May 1784 and July 1787 he flogged 86 of his 334 sailors. And when he got home he had his arm around another man's wife – his girlfriend was Lady Emma Hamilton. That was a bit of a disgrace. But a bigger disgrace came in battles at Naples, where he allowed French prisoners to be killed. Did he care? No. He said, 'You must hate a Frenchman as you hate the devil.'

✖ Nelson just asked for trouble. He stepped out of his cabin to command the Battle of Trafalgar. He was wearing his flashy uniform and bling medals. The enemy gunners had a clear target. They didn't miss. Nelson's corpse was carried home in a barrel of brandy so it didn't rot. It was said the sailors drank the brandy through a straw. But that horrible story is probably NOT true.

## LORD NELSON'S TOP WEAPON:
**CANNON** – Nelson's ship, 'The Victory', had over 100.

to Lord Nelson – with love from the French

# GENERAL GEORGE ARMSTRONG CUSTER (1839–1876)

Warriors need a reason to take risks. Some do it for love of their country. Some do it because they love themselves.

## FIGHTING FACTS

✖ George Custer was famous for getting himself killed. In 1876 Custer led his 256 US soldiers into a battle with Sioux, Cheyenne and Arapahoe warriors. The battle took place at the Little Bighorn River. Custer expected to massacre a few Indians. Instead his troops were massacred. It became known as Custer's Last Stand.

✖ Custer was a bit of a show-off. He wore his golden hair in long ringlets and he dressed in shiny boots and tight trousers. Custer was sure that he was good enough to win the day when he spotted some Sioux at the Little Bighorn. He grabbed the closest troop of soldiers and attacked straight away. He didn't realize that he was outnumbered three to one, and that he should have waited for the rest of his army to arrive.

✖ Custer's troops shot their own horses and then hid behind them for cover, so they had nothing to escape on. They were massacred by Sioux Indians led by Crazy Horse – one Horse they failed to shoot. Custer was shot in the head and the heart, probably by bullets from his own troop's rifles. They were taken from the soldiers' corpses by the Sioux and turned against Custer.

✖ The Sioux were desperate to get their tomahawks on General George Custer's famous long blond scalp. But he'd had his hair cut before he set off. So, while many of his soldiers were scalped after the massacre, Custer wasn't. The haircut confused the Indians. They didn't recognize him. Custer always wanted to be famous. His wife wrote books about him. He became dead famous.

## GENERAL CUSTER'S TOP WEAPON:
### SPRINGFIELD CARBINE RIFLE
— used by the 7th Cavalry to kill Native Americans.

to Custer – with love from the Sioux

# CRAZY CRIMINALS

**C**rime has its own horrible history. There are some crimes, and some punishments, that we don't have today.

## ALCIBIADES – GREEK GENERAL (450–404 BC)

Some people do odd things when they are upset. They go round smashing things…

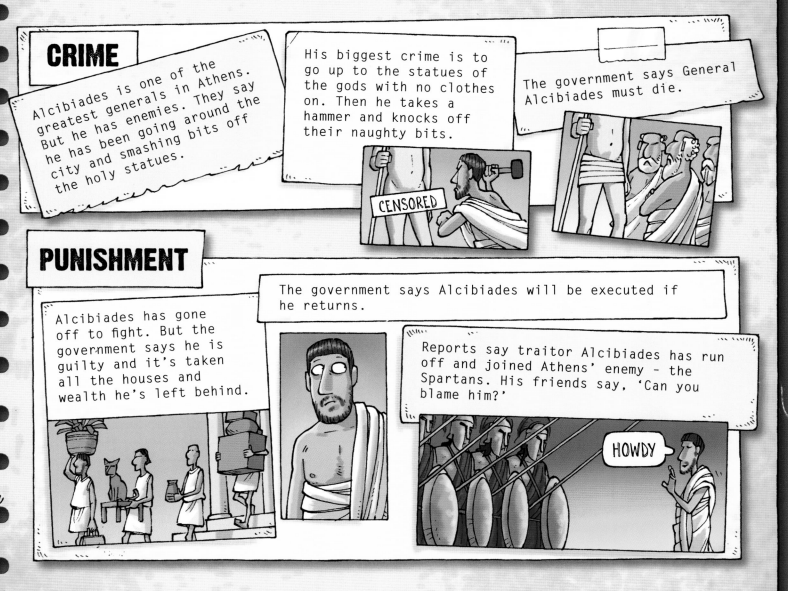

**CRIME**

Alcibiades is one of the greatest generals in Athens. But he has enemies. They say he has been going around the city and smashing bits off the holy statues.

His biggest crime is to go up to the statues of the gods with no clothes on. Then he takes a hammer and knocks off their naughty bits.

CENSORED

The government says General Alcibiades must die.

**PUNISHMENT**

Alcibiades has gone off to fight. But the government says he is guilty and it's taken all the houses and wealth he's left behind.

The government says Alcibiades will be executed if he returns.

Reports say traitor Alcibiades has run off and joined Athens' enemy – the Spartans. His friends say, 'Can you blame him?'

HOWDY

Alcibiades' friends the Spartans killed him in the end. They set fire to his house. When he ran out they shot him down in a shower of arrows. (This hurts even more than having your naughty bits knocked off.)

# POPE FORMOSUS (AD 816–896)

Some crimes are curious. But some punishments are crazier than the crimes.

## CRIME

Pope Formosus is a disgrace. He is moving bishops around like pieces on a chessboard. Church law does not allow this.

The evil Pope Formosus has told the German King Arnulf to invade Italy! Who will stop wicked Formosus?

Formosus is dead and buried. But we haven't heard the last of his crime time as pope.

## PUNISHMENT

New Pope Stephen VI has decided Pope Formosus must go on trial. Even though he is dead!

Formosus has been dug up, dressed in his pope gown and hat then sat on his throne. The trial has started.

AS WELL AS YOUR OTHER DIABOLICAL CRIMES I ACCUSE YOU OF BEING REALLY SMELLY

Formosus has been found guilty. His gown has been ripped to shreds. The fingers he used to bless people have been torn off. The corpse has been thrown in the River Tiber.

The body of Formosus was dragged from the river by a monk – nice job. But the trial of the corpse was not popular. Soon it was Pope Stephen VI's turn to be thrown into prison. He was then strangled. Formosus would have been happy about that!

# ALICE ARDEN – MURDERESS (1516–1551)

Some criminals just go on and on till they get what they want … even if it takes them years.

## CRIME

Rich Thomas Arden has been found dead in a field. Murdered. The killers hoped a snowstorm would cover up their tracks, but the snow stopped and the law has tracked them.

The killers of Thomas Arden are two villains called Black Will and George Loosebag. Law officers are trying to find out why they would murder poor Arden.

Black Will

Loosebag

Black Will and Loosebag have spilled the beans. They were asked to murder Arden by his wife, Alice. They smashed him over the head with an iron. Alice Arden then made sure he was dead with seven or eight stabs of a knife. It seems she wanted rid of Thomas so she could marry her new boyfriend.

## PUNISHMENT

Black Will and George Loosebag have been put on trial and found guilty. They say they were offered ten pounds for the murder. They also robbed the corpse and will hang for their crime.

A new witness says Alice Arden has been planning to murder her husband for TWO YEARS. She bought poison and put it in his food. When it failed she turned to Black Will and Loosebag.

Alice Arden is guilty. But she will not hang. Hanging is too good for her. A woman who kills her husband is guilty of 'treason'. She faces a much more gruesome death. She will be burned at the stake. Large crowds will gather to watch the end of awful Alice.

The law had just about everyone executed. Even Alice Arden's maid was sentenced to death. Like Alice, the maid was burned alive. She was not happy and went to the stake saying some very nasty things about Alice Arden. Well, you would, wouldn't you?

# ANDREW MERRILEES – BODY-SNATCHER (BORN AROUND 1790)

If the law doesn't catch criminals then the ordinary people will take the law into their own hands.

## CRIME

Our reports say a leading body-snatcher is merry Andrew Merrilees. He is a tall man, about 6 ft 4 in and he is so skinny that his clothes sort of hang loose on him. Our loved ones are not safe in their graves.

Edinburgh has a new type of crime. Men are going around stealing bodies from their graves. They sell the corpses to the doctors to cut up in the teaching hospitals. Who are these mystery body-snatchers?

A row has broken out among the body-snatchers. Andrew's sister has died and a rival gang said they'd steal the body. But Andrew got there first, dug up his sister and sold her for ten pounds. How sick is that?

YOU SAID I WAS DEAD SPECIAL

I SAID SPECIAL DEAD

## PUNISHMENT

Stealing a corpse is not seen as a great crime! If you are caught you will only get a fine or a short spell in prison. No one has caught merry Andrew Merrilees and some think they never will. He is just too crafty.

Word has gone around that Professor Robert Knox is the man who buys the corpses from the grave-robbers. The law cannot prove this so the Edinburgh mob has attacked his house and smashed all the windows.

THERE'S NO BODY HERE GEDDIT?

Professor Robert Knox, the corpse-cutter, has died in London. He was driven from Edinburgh by the hatred of the mob. Now he is buried (safely) in an unmarked grave. The body-snatchers have escaped punishment.

Professor Robert Knox was never found guilty of a crime. But he suffered more than the men like Merrilees who dug up the corpses. The mob made a dummy of him, hanged it from a tree and set fire to it. Knox had to leave Edinburgh and for a while made a living selling books on fishing.

Knox was a great teacher. Visitors to his hospital told how they met him *'dressed in a hospital gown and with bloody fingers'*. And you thought YOUR teachers were bad...

# NED KELLY - OUTLAW (1855–1880)

Some criminals become heroes in their own land. They fight for the people against the cruel law.

## CRIME

Constable Alexander Fitzpatrick, has been attacked at the Kelly home on Eleven Mile Creek. He says he went there to arrest Ned's brother Dan for horse-stealing. Fitzpatrick was attacked by a number of the Kelly clan, then shot in the wrist by Ned. This makes Ned Kelly an outlaw.

PING
PING!
PING-PING!
SPLAT!

Police hunting the Kelly gang have been ambushed at Stringybark Creek. Three policemen have been shot and the Kelly gang will hang if they are caught.

There has been a hotel siege at Glenrowan, where on 28 June 1880 three members of the Kelly gang were shot dead. Ned wore a suit of body armour made from a steel plough. He forgot to wear armour on his legs though. That's where the police shot him.

## PUNISHMENT

In Melbourne on 28 October 1880 outlaw Ned Kelly was tried for the murder of Constable Thomas Lonigan at Stringybark Creek. Kelly said he was defending himself, *'I had to shoot them, or lie down and let them shoot me, scattering pieces of me and my brother all over the bush.'*

Outlaw Ned Kelly has been found guilty of murder. He will be hanged at the Melbourne gaol on 11 November. The judge said Kelly would go to Hell. Kelly said, *'I'll see you there, then!'*

As they put the rope around his neck to hang him, Kelly said, *'Ah well, I suppose it had to come to this. Such is life.'* Then he died. Now that's cool. Stupid ... but cool.

Ned Kelly did not like the police. He said they were *'a brutal and cowardly parcel of big ugly fat-necked wombat-headed, big bellied, magpie-legged, narrow-hipped, splay-footed sons of English landlords'*.

# Torturers' Tales

**S**ometimes people don't do what you want them to – ask any teacher. That's when you have to give them a little pain.

## Tiberius – Emperor of Rome (42 BC–AD 37)

Being a Roman emperor can be hard work. So it's nice to take a break – take and break a leg, an arm, a skull – that sort of thing…

### TERRIBLE TORTURER'S TOUGH TALK

*I don't care if they hate me … so long as they obey me!*

WE WILL DO WHATEVER YOU SAY

YOU VILE STINKY TOAD

### TERRIBLE TORTURER'S HORRIBLEST HABIT

Breaking the legs of anyone who upset him.

WOW! YOU MUST HAVE UPSET TIBERIUS A *LOT*!

NOPE … I FELL OFF MY HORSE

### TERRIBLE TORTURER'S TWISTED TALE

**E**mperor Tiberius needed a holiday. 'I think I'll take a break!' he cried. His servants ran off to find their shin pads and he groaned, 'No, I mean a holiday. A short break on the island of Capri off the south coast of Italy would be very nice.'

He had only been there three days when a humble Capri fisherman caught a large crab and a huge mullet fish. 'This will make a wonderful gift for our guest, the emperor!' he smiled.

The cliff was steep and there was no track. The mullet was heavy. The fisherman struggled for an hour and finally reached the top. 'Take me to the emperor,' he begged the guard.

'The emperor wishes to be left alone today,' the guard said with a shake of the head. 'It's the biggest mullet I've ever caught,' the fisherman said proudly. 'The gods must have meant it for the emperor. Tell the emperor I must see him!'

The guard shrugged. It was a boring life, standing on the top of the cliff, watching the sea birds. The emperor might order him to break the fisherman's legs. 'I'll see what the emperor says,' he said with a secret smirk.

Five minutes later he returned and said with a grin, 'Emperor Tiberius will see you now.'

The poor little fisherman dragged the huge

fish into the emperor's room. 'You'll be sorry,' the guard muttered.

As the fisherman stepped through the door, two huge guards grabbed his arms. 'I've brought a gift for the emperor!' he squawked.

Emperor Tiberius stepped forward. 'You disturbed my rest, you smelly little man,' he snarled.

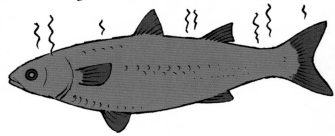

'It's the fish, your worship...' the little man explained.

'No,' the emperor jeered. 'The fish smells sweeter than you.' Then he roared, 'Guard!'

'Yes, sir?'

'Sweeten the little man. Rub that fish over his body.'

'It was a present ... ouch! ... Mullet scales are very rough!' the fisherman screamed.

The guard scrubbed the rough skin over the fisherman's face till it was left raw and bleeding. The guard smiled as he then started to strip the skin off the fisherman's chest.

'Ahhhh! Ooooh!' the man wailed.

'Enough!' the emperor snapped. The guards let the fisherman fall to the floor, where he lay groaning and muttering something though his bleeding lips.

'What did you say?' Tiberius growled.

'I said, thank the gods I didn't bring you that crab I caught this morning,' the little man babbled.

The emperor's eyes lit up with an evil glee. 'Go to this man's house and fetch the crab,' he ordered.

The guard nodded. As he left the emperor's room he winked at the sobbing fisherman. 'I said that you'd be sorry.'

And, after being scrubbed with the sharp shell of the crab, the fisherman was so sorry he wished he had never been born.

## STICKY END

Emperor Tiberius died at the age of 78. Some say he was smothered by his chief servant. Others say he was slowly poisoned by the next emperor, Caligula.

The Roman people went wild with happiness. They ran by the River Tiber where the corpses of criminals were thrown. They chanted...

INTO THE TIBER WITH TIBERIUS

It's a joke, you see? (But not a very good one.)

# PHILIP IV – KING OF FRANCE (1268–1314)

One kruel king used torture to get out of paying back the money he owed.

## TERRIBLE TORTURER'S TOUGH TALK

ANYONE WHO DISOBEYS THE CHURCH IS A 'HERETIC' AND THE PUNISHMENT IS TO BE BURIED ALIVE

WE WILL DO WHATEVER HE SAYS

## TERRIBLE TORTURER'S HORRIBLEST HABIT

In 1231 Pope Gregory IX had chosen monks to go around looking for 'heretics'. Thousands were tortured and burned. But one group of monks became knights – warrior monks who called themselves Knights Templar.

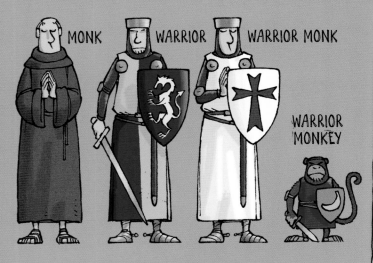

MONK  WARRIOR  WARRIOR MONK  WARRIOR 'MONKEY'

They became rich – and where there is money there are jealous people. Eighty years after Gregory started the search it was the Templars who faced the torturers…

## TERRIBLE TORTURER'S TWISTED TALE

The Grand Master of the knights was tall and his eyes burned like a fire. His face was grim but he tried to smile at the French king. 'Good evening, Your Majesty,' he said.

King Philip said, 'It's morning, Jacques de Molay, it's morning.'

De Molay shrugged. 'I've been in your torture chamber so long I have lost track of time.'

'Torture chamber?' the king said and blinked as if he were puzzled. 'This is my guest room. My servants here want you to talk to them. They want you to tell them the truth. Oh, they may have stretched your body out on the rack until you begged for mercy– but all they want is the truth.'

De Molay shook his head. 'The truth is you owe my knights, the Knights Templar, a fortune. You think that if you arrest me then you will not have to pay. But my knights will not let you get away with it.'

King Philip pushed his face close to the prisoner's. 'Wrong. On Friday 13th March we didn't just arrest you. We arrested every single Knight Templar in the kingdom. They will talk or they will be tortured. They will be found guilty and executed. All of your gold will be mine, Jacques de Molay.'

The knight was chained close to the wall but he managed to pull back his head a little way then jerk it forward and spit in King Philip's handsome face.

The king turned to the soldier beside him. 'Put this heretic back on the strappado. Hurt him till he confesses.'

The man started to unfasten the chains. He mumbled. 'He won't talk.'

'He'll talk for me,' Philip hissed and watched as the weak knight was carried across the cell and placed on wooden blocks. He had his arms tied behind his back. A rope was fastened to his wrists and thrown over a beam till it was tight.

Philip kicked away the top block. De Molay dropped.

De Molay's arms were torn at the shoulders. De Molay gasped. His toes took a little of his weight on the last block.

Philip walked round the hanging man. 'We have had reports that the Templars are enemies of the true Church,' he said.

'A lie,' the knight groaned. Philip nodded. He kicked away the final block. The knight screamed.

Philip went on quickly, 'Pope Clement himself is with me. There are 127 charges, including spitting and peeing on the golden cross of Jesus...'

'Never!'

'Worshipping a mysterious head...'

'Ridiculous!'

'... and devil worship! How do you plead?'

'Not guilty!'

The rack tightened, an arm was torn out of its socket and de Molay whispered, 'If you say so!'

Philip smiled. 'You must go to prison for life – and the Templar wealth must be given up ... to me!' He turned to the soldier. 'Release him.'

The guard carried the knight to a wooden bench and laid him down. As Philip began to leave, the prisoner cried, 'You are a liar – we are not guilty!'

Philip stopped and turned. 'Ah, de Molay. I am so pleased to hear that. You see if you confess, the punishment is prison. But if you later CHANGE your mind, then Pope Gregory IX's law says the punishment is death. You'll burn at the stake along with the rest of your gang.' He walked out.

And so it happened that de Molay and many other Templars were taken to the stake on 18 March 1314. They were condemned to die in agony over a slow fire.

As the flames leapt up, the knight cried to Philip, 'I shall meet you and Pope Clement by God's seat before a year is past. You and your family, for thirteen generations, will be cursed!'

The flames did their work. De Molay fell silent. Philip IV laughed at de Molay's curse and went to count his money.

## STICKY END

A month after the execution of the Templars Pope Clement died. Seven months later the torturing King Philip followed him to the grave just as de Molay said he would.

Philip died during a hunt when he was ripped apart by a wild boar.

I'M BOARED

Some terrible torturers couldn't even come up with their own torture ideas – they just borrowed someone else's.

## TERRIBLE TORTURER'S TWISTED TALE

John Holland, the second Duke of Exeter, trotted through the dark, damp passages of the Tower of London, then down a twisting stairway into a dismal dungeon.

The noise of pounding hammers filled the room and the smoke from the torches made the air thick and choking. But John Holland was happy.

A carpenter looked up from the machine he was working on. The sour smell of his sweat made the room even more sickening but John Holland just grinned. 'Finished?' he asked.

'Nearly, Your Grace. I just need to fasten the ropes,' the carpenter explained.

'Let me help you,' the duke said, and walked over to the strange machine. The carpenter passed some coarse ropes to the duke and showed him where to tie them.

'Now then, Your Grace,' the carpenter said, 'this bit in the middle is like a strong bed. I've built many beds in my time and this is just the same ... only longer.'

'My guests won't be getting much sleep,' the duke giggled as he finished tying the ropes.

'The ... erm ... prisoner, lies down here,' the carpenter said.

'Show me.'

The carpenter frowned but lay down stiffly on the boards. 'The prisoner stretches his hands above his head ... like this ... and your torturer fastens a rope round each wrist.'

'Let's see if it works,' the duke said, tying the ropes quickly. 'I suppose the other ropes at the bottom go round your ankles?'

'Yes, Your Grace,' the carpenter said, wheezing with the effort. 'Now ... here's the clever bit. The ropes on my wrists are fastened to a roller. Just push that lever to turn the roller and make the rope go tight.'

'Like this?' John Holland hissed and pushed the lever.

'No! No! No!' the carpenter cried. 'You'll hurt me. No ... ouch – careful ... ohhh ... steady ... ouch ... Your Grace. I'll wet myself if you don't stop.'

The carpenter was fat when he was standing up, but he was stretched so long he looked lean as a greyhound. 'It works,' the duke smiled.

'Yes ... now ... push the lever back. My arms are aching. Any further and you'll rip them out of their sockets ... or my leg joints will get pulled apart. Please, Your Grace! Please.'

'A labourer is worthy of his hire,' the duke nodded.

'What?'

'The Bible says that. You did a good job. You shall be paid. How much did we say?'

'Twenty pounds, sir.'

The duke stroked his beard. 'I'll give you two

pounds. I mean ... I got the plans. I copied the idea from a torture machine in France. The Tower gave you the wood.'

'It took me two weeks to build,' the carpenter argued.

'Two pounds.'

'I can't take less than ten,' the carpenter groaned.

'Can't?' the duke asked and pushed the lever. 'Can't?!'

'Ouch ... you'll kill me ... ouch ... five pounds then. Five!'

John Holland pushed the lever back, slipped the ropes off the man's wrists and pulled him off the rack. The carpenter struggled to stand up on his stretched and shaking legs. The duke reached into a purse and pulled out a small golden coin. 'There you are!'

'We said five,' the carpenter scowled.

'I said two.'

'This is ONE!'

'Yes, I know,' John Holland shrugged. 'I was going to pay you TWO for a NEW torture rack.'

'It IS a new torture rack!' the carpenter cried.

'No ... I've just used it. Would you like me to use it again?' The duke asked. His eyes glittered in the torchlight. He picked up the carpenter's tool bag and thrust it into the man's aching arms.

The carpenter clutched at his coin and stumbled up the stairs towards the grey daylight. The sound of the Duke of Exeter's cackling laugh followed him.

## FOUL FACT

THE RACK IN THE TOWER OF LONDON WAS A COPY OF THE FRENCH ONES. JOHN HOLLAND, DUKE OF EXETER, TOOK OVER AS CONSTABLE OF THE TOWER IN 1447. HE HAD THE RACK BUILT FOR PRISONERS.
THE TOWER TORTURERS HAD A PET NAME FOR THE CRUEL MACHINE ... 'THE DUKE OF EXETER'S DAUGHTER'.
IT WAS USED ON PRISONERS FOR THE NEXT 200 YEARS. IT WAS EVEN USED ON A WOMAN, ANNE ASKEW, IN 1546. SHE WAS A CHURCH REBEL. SHE REFUSED TO TALK AND NAME THE OTHER REBELS.
ANNE SAID...

*Master Rich the torturer put me on the rack till I was nearly dead… When I was set loose I fainted. They woke me up and then put me on the rack again…*

COME ALONG ALICE

A LONG ALICE ... VERY FUNNY

ANNE ASKEW WAS STRETCHED SO MUCH SHE COULDN'T WALK. SHE WAS CARRIED OUT OF THE TOWER TO SMITHFIELD AND BURNED ALIVE.

# JAMES VI OF SCOTLAND (JAMES I OF ENGLAND) (1566–1625)

It's no fun for a king to just give orders to a torturer. He wants to be there to join in the fun!

## TERRIBLE TORTURER'S TOUGH TALK

James hated pipe-smoking. He wrote about the habit and said:

> An oily kind of soot has been found in some great tobacco takers, when they were cut open after their death.

UURGHH

## TERRIBLE TORTURER'S HORRIBLEST HABIT

A visitor said:

> His tongue was too large for his mouth which made him drink very badly as if eating his drink which came out into the cup from each side of his mouth.

# TERRIBLE TORTURER'S TWISTED TALE

*Scotland, 1591*

King James picked his nose. (He did that a lot.) He wiped his glove on his sleeve and sniffed. 'We are here to torture witches,' he said in his whining Scottish voice.

'Excuse me, sir,' the little torturer with the smoke-black hands said. 'We are here to torture people. They may confess to being witches – or they may not. If they are NOT then we aren't torturing witches.'

King James's eyes bulged like boiled gooseberries. 'Yes, Master Plank, you are right ... but if you torture them well, they WILL confess.'

'Seems a bit harsh, if you don't mind me saying so', the grimy little man shrugged.

The king licked his blubbery, red lips and said, 'Master Plank. I married Princess Anne of Denmark...'

'Fine lady, sir. Fine lady.'

'And what happened to the fine lady when she sailed from Denmark to marry me?' the king whined.

'Storms drove her back, they say, sir.'

'Storms drove her back. And when I went to Denmark myself to bring her home to Scotland, what happened to us?'

'More storms, sir.'

'Yes!' the king cried. 'And WHY have Anne and I suffered so many storms? I'll tell you why. The captain of our ship said the storms were whipped up by witches. Witches at North Berwick.'

'They must have used a big whip!' the torturer laughed.

'They dug a corpse out of the graveyard, cut off its hands and tied them to the paws of a cat. They threw the cat into the sea and that caused the storm,' the king told him. 'The girl Gilly Duncan told us.'

The torturer sighed. 'She was fastened to the walls of a cell and had an iron mask on her face. Sharp prongs were pushed into her mouth. She would tell you anything just to escape the pain.'

The king paced up and down the cell, rubbing a hand under his dripping nose. 'She told us the leader of the group was this schoolteacher, John Fian.'

'Yes, sir, so we tortured him.'

'How?' James asked and his gooseberry eyes glowed.

'We used thumbscrews to crush his fingers...'

'The pilliwinks, we call them,' James nodded.

'Then, when his nails fell out, we pushed pins up his fingertips as far as they'd go. He howled with pain but he didn't own up to being a witch.'

'Good! Good!' James chuckled. 'And did you try the boot?'

'Yes, sir. We put the iron boot on his leg then drove wedges in till his shin was squeezed,' Master Plank nodded.

'Aye, but were the bones crushed? Did the leg spout blood?' King James cried.

'No, sir, we didn't go that far.'

'Good! Good! Then you can try it now. But this time I will be here. This time we'll have blood and we will make him confess. Bring in the teacher!'

'Yes, sir,' the torturer said, and went to the door of the cell. He looked through the bars. 'You have a very important visitor, Mister Fian!' he called.

'That's good!' the teacher called back.

'Oh, no it's not,' Master Plank sighed. 'Oh, no it's not.'

## FOUL FACT

**TEACHER FIAN WAS TORTURED WITH THE BOOT TILL HE COULDN'T WALK. KING JAMES WATCHED AND ENJOYED IT. FIAN WAS THEN SENT TO BE EXECUTED. A REPORT SAID...**

Fian was put into a cart, and carried to the place of execution. First he was strangled, then he was immediately put into a great fire, being ready for him. He was burned in the Castle Hill of Edinburgh on a Saturday in the end of January 1591.

Another North Berwick witch was called Agnes Sampson. It was said that she used black-magic spells...

• Making 'corpse-powder' for spells from dead bodies and grease from the fat of a dead child
• Talking with devils and fairies
• Changing the weather and making storms
• Causing death and disease in enemies
• Having mole's feet in her purse so it was always full of silver

Agnes was executed on the same day as John Fian and three others. One of them was Gilly Duncan – the foolish girl who had reported the North Berwick witches.

Agnes, an old woman, had been tortured. She was 'thawed' – a rope was wrapped around her head and twisted till it became tighter and tighter, crushing her skull. Some people thought you could kill someone with black magic. Take some stale pee, mix it with the juices from a crushed toad and feed it to the victim. Yummy.

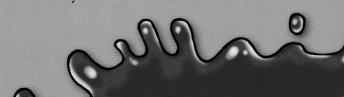

# REINHARD TRISTAN EUGEN HEYDRICH – GERMAN GENERAL (1904–1942)

Sometimes torture is used to discover your enemy's secrets – but the rest of the world will hate you for it.

## TERRIBLE TORTURER'S TOUGH TALK

Heydrich didn't want to get the blame when his enemies were arrested. He wanted them to just disappear. So he said:

> *I want people to be captured and killed under the cover of night and fog.*

## TERRIBLE TORTURER'S HORRIBLEST HABIT

Having his friends executed. Heydrich got on well with Ernst Rohm, and they were friends for 14 years. But when they fell out Heydrich went to Adolf Hitler and said, 'Rohm is part of a plot to kill you!' So, of course, Hitler had Rohm executed – shot in the head. Rotten Reinhard.

## TERRIBLE TORTURER'S TWISTED TALE

*Prague, Czech Republic, 1942*

The torturer lay on a hospital bed. He had said goodbye to his wife and now he was slipping slowly towards death. The pain was over. The pain was just about to begin for hundreds more.

Doctor Gebhart looked at him. 'He should not be dying. If I had been here when he was wounded I would have saved him.'

The other doctors looked at their feet and didn't speak. The army guards smirked. Doctor Gebhart glared at them through his glinting spectacles. 'And you soldiers are as much to blame!' he raged. 'Reinhard Heydrich was your leader. Your job was to protect him.'

'We tried,' the colonel muttered. 'Heydrich took the same route every day. The assassins knew that. Anyone with any sense would have made sure he took a different road at a different time every day. All they had to do was wait at that sharp bend at Holesovice. They knew the car would slow down and make an easy target.'

'I had to slow down,' the driver said.

The doctor gave a short laugh. 'But you didn't have to stop. The first assassin jumped on to the car with his machine gun and pulled the trigger. It didn't fire. He'd forgotten to take off the safety catch – the clown! Heydrich fired his own pistol as the man ran away. What did you do?'

'Stopped the car and ran after him,' the driver said.

'Yes. If you had driven away then, at full speed, your master would have been saved.

Idiot! There was a second assassin – there always is. He threw a hand grenade and blew in the back of the car. Splinters of metal and pieces of the car seat were blasted into Heydrich's back. But they didn't kill him, did they?' Now Doctor Gebhart turned on the Prague doctors.

'No, Professor,' they muttered.

'No, Professor. You failed to clean the wounds properly. The wounds turned poisonous. By the time our leader Adolf Hitler sent me here I was already too late to save Heydrich. He is not dying from an assassin's bomb. He is dying from a piece of dirty car seat in his spleen. Idiots. He is dying in terrible pain. Make sure the Czech people feel the same sort of pain.'

He turned back to the pale-faced, fair-haired man on the bed. He was breathing his last.

Doctor Gebhart walked across to the colonel. 'The orders from Herr Hitler are that you are

to do everything to track down and execute the assassins. Everything. Herr Hitler says that anyone who helped the murderers is to be tortured and shot along with everyone in his family. Do not be gentle when you question the people of Prague.'

'Torture?'

'Of course! You are the Gestapo. The Gestapo that Reinhard Heydrich led. He knew that we have to give a little pain to the enemies of the Nazis. A little pain to get them to talk. Heydrich is not a cruel man. But our enemies must suffer so we can live. Do it!'

The colonel clicked his heels and bowed. 'Yes, Professor. We shall enjoy that.'

As the great torturer lay on his bed and breathed his last, his army of torturers set about their ruthless job.

# FOUL FACT

NO ONE IN PRAGUE BETRAYED THE ASSASSINS, KUBIS AND GABCIK. THEN THE GESTAPO FOUND A CLUE THAT LED THEM TO A FAMILY WHO HAD GIVEN SHELTER TO THE ASSASSINS. THE FAMILY WAS TORTURED. KUBIS AND GABCIK WERE TRACED TO THEIR HIDING PLACE – A CHURCH IN PRAGUE. THE NAZIS SURROUNDED THE CHURCH AND A GUN BATTLE BEGAN. TEAR GAS FAILED TO GET THE ASSASSINS OUT. THEY HID IN THE CELLARS. THE NAZIS CALLED IN THE CZECH FIRE BRIGADE TO FLOOD THE CELLARS. THE ASSASSINS WERE BROUGHT OUT DEAD. THEY HAD USED THEIR LAST BULLETS TO SHOOT THEMSELVES.

THE CZECH PEOPLE SUFFERED HORRIBLY. A GESTAPO FORCE SURROUNDED THE TOWN OF LIDICE. EVERY MAN WAS TAKEN AND SHOT. THE WOMEN AND CHILDREN WERE SENT TO PRISON CAMPS. THE TOWN WAS BURNED TO THE GROUND AS A LESSON TO THE CZECH PEOPLE.

REINHARD TRISTAN EUGEN HEYDRICH, THE GREAT TORTURER, WAS DEAD. BUT HIS GESTAPO TORTURE GANG WAS JUST STARTING.

NAZI TORTURES INCLUDED...

- FREEZING A VICTIM TILL THEY WERE NEARLY DEAD
- DUCKING SOMEONE'S FACE IN AN ICY BATH TILL THEY NEARLY DROWNED
- BURNING THE SKIN WITH MATCHES
- ELECTRIC SHOCKS
- BEATING WITH RUBBER STICKS (PAINFUL BUT LEFT NO MARKS)

STRANGELY, THE GESTAPO USED THE STRAPPADO ... HANGING SOMEONE FROM THEIR ARMS STRAPPED BEHIND THEIR BACK ... JUST AS TORTURERS IN THE MIDDLE AGES HAD, MORE THAN 500 YEARS BEFORE.

## ❧ DID YOU KNOW…? ❧

In 1938 Germany's monstrous leader, Adolf Hitler, said…

> Torture? Anything is legal if it gets me what I want.

In 2006 the USA's secret service was found torturing prisoners. The government said its secret agents would not be punished by the law.

Sixty years after the Nazis, nothing has changed. Adolf Hitler would be happy…

# EPILOGUE

There are thousands of famous people. But in history the most famous ones always seem to be a bit nasty. Even the heroes can be horrible. Want to know how they became famous?

YES PLEASE!

Here are just some of the ways. They…

✖ Assassinated a leader – and ended up with their head on a pole!

✖ Told people they were gods … then got strangled.

✖ Did something wild but stupid and got killed making a hopeless attack.

✖ Thought of some new crime, like digging up corpses and selling them.

✖ Or they were just very good at their job – very good at slicing off heads.

You wouldn't want to go down in history for those reasons, would you?

MAYBE NOT

No. You can live a useful life and make everyone around you happy. That's more important than being 'famous'.

HOW DO I DO THAT? ANY IDEAS?

You could tell them stories! Everyone likes a *Horrible Histories* story. Grab your friends, sit them down with a cup of warm blood … or a cup of tea … and tell stories.

HAVE I EVER TOLD YOU THE TALE OF OLD BRUNHILDA … TORN APART BY WILD HORSES?

You may not be famous as Caesar – or as dead as him. But you could be very, very popular! Remember - *Horrible Histories* wins friends.

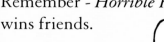

THANKS!

# INTERESTING INDEX

**H**ang on! This isn't one of your boring old indexes. This is a horrible index. It's the only index in the world where you will find bloodsucking leeches, kissing corpses, naughty bits and all the other things you really HAVE to know if you want to be a horrible historian. Read it and creep.